Captivating Your Class
Effective Teaching Skills

JOANNE PHILPOTT

continuum

Continuum International Publishing Group

The Tower Building   80 Maiden Lane
11 York Road   Suite 704
London, SE1 7NX   New York, NY 10038

www.continuumbooks.com

British Library Cataloguing-in-Publication Data
A catalogue record for this book is available from the British Library.

ISBN: 978-1-84706-267-3 (paperback)

Library of Congress Cataloging-in-Publication Data
Philpott, Joanne.
Captivating your class: effective teaching skills / Joanne Philpott.
    p. cm.
Includes bibliographical references.
ISBN 978-1-84706-267-3
1. High school teaching–Great Britain. 2. Effective teaching–Great
    Britain. 3. A-level examinations–Great Britain. I. Title.

LB1607.53.G7P45 2009
373.11–dc22   2008039190

Typeset by Newgen Imaging Systems Pvt Ltd, Chennai, India
Printed and bound in Great Britain by Antony Rowe

Contents

Introduction

This book is based on classroom practice and is designed as a practical resource for teachers of Advanced Level teaching and learning. I began teaching 'A' Level when I was a newly qualified teacher and remember the anxiety induced from planning those lessons. 'A' Level teaching seemed to bear no relation to my 11–16 teaching. I had been given no specialist training just one session during my Post Graduate Certificate in Education (PGCE) course and a few lessons on teaching practice. The department I worked in seemed to view sixth form as a separate entity almost as if this were the 'icing on the cake' or the 'golden child' of teaching and you could simply walk into the classroom and teach. It was simply expected that I could teach sixth form because I had teaching qualification and a degree in the subject I was teaching.

When I became a subject leader I wanted to change this view and make sixth form teaching a part of a bigger 11–19 experience. I wanted teachers and students to gain a sense of progression in their learning, as they moved from Key Stage 3 to General Certificate Secondary Education (GCSE) and onto 'A' Level. My aim was for the students and teachers to make connections across their subject experience and not compartmentalize their studies into boxes determined by examination. I also felt that teachers deserved opportunities for professional development in 'A' Level teaching beyond that of subject-content based conferences and examination board training.

As an advanced skills teacher I resolved to make 'A' Level teaching and learning a focus area and began expanding my post-16 teaching repertoire and developing strategies to help student learning in and out of their lessons. I made use of learning strategies from 11–16 classrooms and talked directly to students about their lessons and their preferred approaches to learning. Their responses were fascinating and demonstrated their desire to take greater ownership of the way they learn. Many students felt that they were told what to do, how to work and even what to think and never really engaged with their subject and the learning process.

Since delivering In Service Training (INSET) on post-16 teaching and learning I have worked with many 'A' Level teachers who are proud of their creativity in 11–16 classrooms yet are aware they revert to didactic and teacher led lesson structures and delivery in their 'A' Level classrooms. They want to change but often are unsure of how to. More commonly they dare not change for fear results will suffer if they do not ensure they have provided all the relevant knowledge for their students. To reassure teachers over this anxiety I emphasize that the results of my students have consistently improved since moving to the approaches outlined in this book.

In the period since Curriculum 2000 was introduced the spate of government-driven initiatives have left many teachers dealing with what appear to be competing agendas. Due to examination changes and the introduction of key skills, post-16 education has in some instances been largely left untouched by education programmes such as the National Strategy, thinking skills, learning to learn, assessment for learning and others. Yet this book will argue that in all instances post-16 students will benefit from the effective use of the aforementioned strategies and more importantly to the benefit not the detriment of subject knowledge and content.

The aim of the book is two fold. First, it offers practical approaches to teaching in an 'A' Level classroom, this includes AS, A2 and all level 3 equivalents as well as the International Baccalaureate and other post-16 qualifications. The book is primarily designed to give confidence to teachers to teach in a way that encourages students to enjoy learning in their 'A' Level lessons in a purposeful way. In all instances the book refers to teaching in a 'classroom'; however I am aware that a classroom for many teachers is a studio, a playing field or another area that does not meet the traditional definition of a classroom. My definition encompasses all these learning spaces and refers to the physical space in which you teach.

Secondly, it will build on theoretical work where appropriate to help reflection and planning by individual teachers for their specific subjects and classes. 'There is nothing so practical as a good theory,' [Kurt Lewin (1952)] and it is necessary to explore the theoretical base of some of the ideas presented in the book. The references section will guide you to further reading for each of the chapters if you wish to explore the theory in greater depth. The book is in six chapters, each with a different focus and is applicable to all teachers of post-16 students. There is no need to start at the beginning but turn to the chapter that interests you the most first and work on techniques suggested. Gradually work through the chapters and experiment with strategies that interest you and develop them in a manner that supports your subject and your students. There is overlap across all the chapters and ideas mentioned in one chapter may be developed in another.

The key messages of the book are two-fold. Personalized planning of lessons is essential, generic lesson plans will not work at 'A' Level and you will need to be aware of the personalities and individual strengths and weaknesses of the students in your class to be able to structure and develop their learning accordingly. Secondly the strategies will be successful when they have been developed in relation to your subject and consolidated to secure subject knowledge and understanding. To this end many suggestions are exemplified through a range of subject examples for both AS and A2.

I would like to formally acknowledge all the teachers and professionals who have helped my teaching to develop and the many 'A' Level students who have shared the classroom with me.

Joanne Philpott 2008

1 | Enlivening 'A' Level teaching and learning

Children who have are having a good time learn much better than those who are miserable.

Sue Palmer, Times Educational Supplement 2002

An 'A' Level classroom is an exciting place to be; no two experiences within it will ever be the same and the students within it will bring out the best in you and occasionally the worst. Students of 'A' Level are different compared to their younger counterparts as they have actively chosen to be in your subject classroom, playing field, laboratory or studio. They spent time making decisions with their family and friends about taking a course of 'A' Levels or level 3 equivalents and then deliberated over which subjects to take. For many this decision will not have been taken lightly. The success of their examinations will determine their immediate future and to some extent the rest of their lives, therefore, they deserve the best learning opportunities available to them. They are eager to learn more but they will also need to learn how to study your subject.

In many ways an 'A' Level classroom is a unique classroom in regard to the nature of the learning that takes place there. Due to examination pressures, 'A' Level classrooms are often knowledge driven with lesson objectives based around syllabus content and understanding of the subject information. Teachers are very aware that the students' understanding will be examined through externally marked AS and A2 papers and this can place a pressure on teachers to emphasize syllabus content through their lesson planning rather than the means by which the knowledge can be learned or conveyed. In other words the content drives the teaching and the pedagogy takes a back seat. Many classroom practitioners excel at key stage 3 and key stage 4 yet feel unable to transfer these skills into an 'A' Level classroom for fear of their students' failing to assimilate enough material for the examination. This book seeks to overcome this fear through considering how an 'A' Level classroom can become a captivating classroom driven by learning and the teacher's and students' enjoyment of the learning that takes place there.

This chapter demonstrates a series of more interesting and innovative strategies to create a positive and challenging learning environment for your students. Some of the techniques will be well-known to you in your 11–16 teaching; if they are recognizable to you they will also be familiar to your students and most people enjoy a sense of security in their learning. Many of the strategies discussed are built around long-practised ideas of active learning, for those readers unfamiliar with this approach to learning this means students have to be involved in their learning through interaction and physical activity rather than passive listening and reading. Techniques are discussed in theoretical and practical terms and exemplified through subject examples. All the strategies have been tried and tested on a range of post-16 students and revised and updated accordingly. A particular practice may not be written for a physics or physical education lesson but with your specialist expertise and a little creativity, an idea can be adapted to suit the needs of a laboratory or a playing field rather than a classroom.

1. Talking

Teachers like to talk; at 'A' Level we love to speak as we can indulge our passion for our subject with a group of students we readily believe are hanging on our every word. AS and A2 students however can be reluctant to enter into discussion and this can lead to the classroom becoming a static environment where learning takes place through the written and not the oral medium. This section will consider the nature of classroom discussion and how the students can become more active participants without losing the necessary depth of knowledge required at post-16 level.

Without question, teacher exposition is a necessary and important classroom tool. It is arguably of greater value within an 'A' Level classroom, where complex subject knowledge needs to be made clear to students if they are to move forward with their learning. Effective teacher explanation requires two key skills; the first to be able to gain and maintain your audiences attention and second to pitch the exposition at the correct level. This can be challenging in an 'A' Level classroom where you have students who achieved GCSE grades ranging from C–A* and have predicted AS and A2 grades from E–A*.

It is important to remember how very mixed in ability an 'A' Level classroom is. Post-16 the majority of teacher talk will be for cognitive rather than procedural or for managerial purposes. The 1992 National Oracy Project suggested that in an 11–16 environment, two-thirds of lessons are talk, two-thirds of that talk is teacher talk and two-thirds of that talk is about management and procedure rather than content. It therefore follows that if there is less procedural or managerial talk there should be less teacher talk as a proportion of the lesson. At 'A' Level the temptation can be to fill the void and talk more about cognitive issues; this can of course be beneficial to the students but look at it in a different way; if you do not need to talk as much then save the most valuable asset you have, that of your voice, and encourage different types of talk between the class as a group and sub-groups within the class.

Speaking in a classroom should be a participatory event. Evidence from the KS3 National Literacy Strategy has proven that learning is increased when students engage in dialogue about their topic or subject. This poses many questions for the teacher to consider when planning dialogue in a lesson.

◆ What can student talk appear like?
◆ How do you plan for it?
◆ How do you ensure all students are involved?
◆ How do you keep talk on task?
◆ When should you interrupt or end the discussion?
◆ How do you assess whether the talk has been purposeful and beneficial to the objectives of the lesson?

Discussion is most effective as a learning process rather than just an activity and will need to be planned for within the broader framework of the lesson. In addition to this; answers to the previous questions will need to be formulated in advance of the lesson in order to maximize the potential of your students. Below are a list of strategies you can use with your students to help develop talking techniques.

Whole class talk

Talk Tokens. Each individual has a given number of talk tokens that they have to use within a discussion. These can be as simple as plastic coins or lollypop sticks or something more creative such as an illustrated laminated card. Students have to aim to use all their tokens within a discussion, they cannot be traded or bargained for, once their tokens are used up they will have to wait for more tokens to become available or write down their comment for later use. Providing a pack of sticky-notes to each group can be helpful to record unheard contributions. For a talkative student who can be prone to dominate the discussion they will have to think before they talk and use their tokens wisely. After a few attempts they will quickly realize that wasting tokens early on in less analytical and cognitive aspects of the discussion will frustrate and impede their learning. You may choose to give a more talkative student fewer tokens to really challenge their use of contributions and listening skills. Handle such an approach with sensitivity. They will hopefully become wise with their words and think much more before they talk.

For a quiet student, having to speak can be an intimidating and overwhelming experience and the teacher needs to be sensitive in handling these students. In the first instances give these students less tokens but make sure there are secure, signposted, opportunities for them to use them. Use directed questioning as an entry route into the discussion and give praise to the student as often as possible. Over time, increase the number of their tokens and remove the scaffold you have provided.

As with any method of learning some students will have their preferences but this approach demonstrates that opting out of discussion is simply not an option. A student would not be allowed to choose to not write up their methodology or demonstrate mathematical working out and equally the benefits of discussing their learning are too great to grant a student the liberty of not contributing to class discussion. A variation of this is to have a talking stick or cuddly toy that is passed around the group whenever someone wishes to speak but you are only allowed a limited number of goes and the same person cannot speak in succession. This can interrupt the flow of discussion but works well in a question and answer style dialogue where the teacher is posing the questions rather than a free-flowing debate.

Extended Talk. Extended talk also encourages each member of the class to contribute and effectively silences the dominant student who simply loves the sound of his or her own voice. The teacher poses the opening question for discussion and students are only allowed to contribute if their response or comment brings a new point to the deliberations. This means that a student cannot repeat or reiterate a statement already made; their contribution has to be new and different and must either challenge, support or extend a comment already made. This can be difficult for students at first and there are often long interludes as students pause for thought. The teacher must be patient and students will get used to this formal style of discussion if used frequently and regularly. This requires the teacher to prepare the questions to be posed in advance to ensure they have the necessary challenge. (See Chapter Three for further discussion of questioning).

A Psychology debate relating to the explanation of criminal behaviour could employ an extended talk technique as many students' may feel the need to reinforce the same point rather than introduce new case studies to extend, counter or conclude upon the arguments raised. Upbringing, cognition and behaviour will all require consideration and extended talk is a way of ensuring coverage and development within the topic. Skills of critical thinking clarity, credibility, accuracy, precision, relevance, depth, breadth, logic, significance and fairness can also demonstrated and assessed through extended talk debate.

Audience Talk. Audience talk is a way of getting students to think about whom they are talking to and who might be listening to their discussion. Many teachers of 'A' Level are used to using audience in written work but do they identify with a sense of audience during classroom dialogue? Ask the students to imagine there is someone in the classroom listening to their dialogue or banter in the lesson and that they must adjust their speech accordingly. For example, it could be someone fun like Granny or little brother or it could be a university lecturer in their subject or a scribe who needs to take notes from the class. Ask the class to consider what impact this would have on the way they talk to you and to each other. Are they speaking in plainer language for the benefits of a younger sibling or using a far more complex vocabulary in order to impress the expert in the field? Either way the use of subject-specific terminology, level of explanation and depth of synthesis will all need to be accounted for and in turn this will raise the importance of classroom dialogue in a student's learning process.

Small group talk

Paired Talk. Paired talk has immense benefit in involving the student who is less keen on speaking in front of the whole group. A teacher will need keen ears and a clearly defined volume control to ensure an acceptable working milieu. There are clear advantages to using small group talk and methods such as 'think, pair, share' can ensure thinking time as well as talking time. With paired talk however it is important not to force students to repeat or summarize the findings of their small group discussion. Not only can this be tedious and time consuming in an 'A' Level classroom but consider what benefits it actually brings to the learning of the students? The teacher should use the time during paired talk to wander around the classroom listening in to the discussion and posing more challenging questions to the small groups who require it. The teacher can take this opportunity to record points of interest that are worthy of whole class discussion and can move the knowledge and understanding of the whole class forward. If talk is unnecessarily repetitive it can become dull and boring and have little value in students' repertoire of learning tools.

It is worth considering at this stage how a teacher might group students and the merits and demerits of mixing abilities against the advantages and disadvantages of matching similar abilities together. Small group discussion is the perfect opportunity for students to develop their oral skills through working with like-minded students. Students are exposed to the vast ability range in an 'A' Level classroom every day so it could be argued why replicate this in a small group discussion environment? Allowing more-able students to extend their thinking further with the challenging dialogue of like-minded students can accelerate their subject skills and encourage the student to think and speak like a mathematician or a geographer instead of a merely a student of maths or geography. Similarly allowing the less-able student to consolidate their learning and ask their own questions will provide this less confident student with the necessary support framework for their learning.

Summary

Participating in discussion is a vital aspect of an 'A' Level classroom and an essential pre-requisite to advanced learning. Yet it is an area in which students can often be reluctant to participate in. Plan a discussion technique into each lesson in order to build student's self- esteem and plan for progression in this area. 'A' Level students are slighter older Year 11's for their first term yet teachers often expect erudite discourse worthy of undergraduate study. In the same way that students are only able to write at an 'A' Level standard through effective teacher planning of writing in the chosen genre and by modelling examples of the intended outcome; classroom talk also needs to be planned for in exactly the same way and by using a variety of well-chosen techniques. This can be enormously exciting and stimulating for everyone involved.

2. Note taking

Consider a sequence of two 'A' Level lessons. The teacher enters the classroom and informs the students of today's topic for discussion. Students are expected to frantically take notes as the teacher indulges in their monologue with the students having no understanding as to why they are taking the notes in the first place other than because they were told to. The lesson ends with the teacher handing out a resource or text book and asking students to take notes from this for next lesson.

Next lesson comes and the topic of note taking is under discussion but the notes themselves are given little value or consideration within the lesson itself. The lesson continues with further note taking from the teacher and concludes with students being set an extended examination based question.

Both lessons are fulfilling the requirements of the 'A' Level specifications and students' are assimilating the required knowledge base in order to pass their exam, so where is the problem? Look again at the two lesson sequence and consider the following questions:

1. From what medium are the students acquiring knowledge?
2. Will the students retain this knowledge?
3. Do the students see value in the activity they are undertaking?
4. How will their note taking skills improve?
5. Will the students become better in the subject?

'Captivating your class,' through note taking may appear to be a contradiction in terms yet it is a pre-requisite of any 'A' Level student's learning repertoire and should therefore be taught in as interesting a way as possible. Through giving thought to which notes are most effective for a given purpose or audience, the students will immediately be involved in the process of note taking thus making it a more reflective and interesting activity. It is usual and necessary for students to take notes in an 'A' Level classroom as notes form the basis of all students work. For an 'A' Level student, their notes serve many purposes. If these purposes can be understood by both teacher and student, the methodology of note taking can be taught in a more interesting and ultimately effective way.

In most instances notes are made for short-term and long-term purposes. In the short term they allow students to sort out ideas of a given topic or methodology and aid planning. Also, in the short term students may require notes to help them sort out and shape their ideas and thinking. These notes are unlikely to be used as a record of learning and their appearance will be radically different to long term notes. Ideas do not come in neat compartmentalized boxes and students' short-term notes do not need to be either. Short-term notes can also be used to aid planning; most writers like to plan before they begin a full draft of an assignment. Each subject will have its own purpose for the use of notes in the short term. For example, in modern foreign languages they can be used for simple vocabulary or to explain a more complex grammatical structure. In Geography they can explain key features of an environmental feature or for capturing evidence gathered on a field study. If students are being set an extended piece of work or assignment they will need to note down key points and ideas they wish to include in their work. The purpose for note taking in this form is very different again and it is likely that long-term notes will be used to support these short-term planning notes. It is unlikely these notes will be retained for future reference and can take a variety of forms which are discussed later in this section.

Long-term notes are used as both a record of learning and to aid understanding. Many of the topics students study in their AS and A2 courses will not be examined until several months after they have studied them. It is therefore important to retain a record of these topics for immediate and future use. If notes are for future use they will be different in appearance from those for immediate use. They will need to be:

♦ legible;
♦ with clear meaning – especially if to record an argument or interpretation;

- titled and subtitled;
- in their own words;
- consistent with abbreviations and make sense in the future;
- referenced – who is the original author and in what context did the author write or speak;
- filed – electronically or on paper;
- relevant – be prepared to disregard notes as their ideas develop from further study.

In addition to this, notes are used to aid understanding.

Students' understanding of a topic will only improve if teachers challenge students to think about and ask questions of the given topic. Understanding is not an organic process which occurs simply because students write something down. Understanding takes place when an individual thinks about and asks questions of the area of study, and is a developmental process which requires interaction with the topic or concept being studied. This may begin with reading, progress with note taking, advance through discussion, move forward through an assignment, and feel secure after revision. Clearly notes underpin several of these stages of development and choosing the appropriate technique will again be crucial to a student's progression. The process of note taking remains the same however, irrespective of the subject they are being used for.

Styles of notes

Everyone learns differently and every learner will have note taking preferences. In order to make the process more interesting for students it is essential to teach students a variety of approaches to taking notes and by occasionally encouraging them to work outside of their 'comfort zone' and experiment with techniques that are unfamiliar to them so they will be kept alert and focused in the classroom rather than passive and functional. Enabling students to use a different technique and introducing a variety of techniques over a given time period will ensure an element of surprise in the classroom and ensure students remain attentive and challenged. Content can still be delivered, however the emphasis is on the note taking technique thus adding a different dimension to the lesson and a small element of surprise. Debriefing of note taking techniques and their relative effectiveness will be as central to the lesson as the topic the notes were on. Before determining which methods to share with students, consider the following questions:

1. What is the purpose of the notes? See above.
2. From what medium are the notes being taken? See below.
3. Which method of note taking is going to be used given the purpose for making them? See below.
4. Have the students used this method before? If yes, how will you ensure progression? See Chapter Four.
5. Are you going to model the method for the students? If so, are you going to use a previous student's work or your own?
6. How will you help the student improve in this method? For example, have you planned to revisit this technique in a future lesson? See Chapter Three.

Below is a description of suggested methods of note taking you can use with your students.

Summary Notes. These are condensed version of the original text and are often in prose. They can be easy to write and do not require much engagement with the original text. They can be useful as a first set of long-term notes and may benefit from highlighting the key words afterwards or listing key words next to them as might appear on a web page as hyper links.

Bullet Points. Probably the most popular form of notes and possibly the least inspired. They should encourage students to keyword and use headings and subheadings. They are effective for speed and when recording a lecture or discussion. Careful consideration of their use must be given as students have a tendency to miss out more in-depth points in their quest to cut information down.

Graphic Organizers. 'Graphic organizers' appears to be a growth industry with a plethora of techniques to organize thinking being marketed and easily found on the internet. Venn diagrams, KWL charts (these are charts where a student fills in what they already Know, what they Want to know, and after the task what they have Learned), mind maps and fishbone diagrams are just a few. They are thinking-skills tools and ensure students are processing their knowledge and understanding effectively.

Pictorial Prompts. For learners with a visual memory, pictorial prompts can be useful as a trigger to further information. This is especially useful when creating notes for revision purposes. The images and symbols that are used need only make sense to the author and it requires thought to create the images and pictures which aid such notes. Designing an image which draws together a range of events and ideas can be an effective front page to a set of notes and make students examine significance, factors, links and other more challenging questions within your course.

Taking notes from different media

To keep a classroom interesting and accessible to all students there must be a variety of stimuli and media from which the students can learn. The teacher is by definition the subject specialist and should be the students' first learning resource. Text books often run a close second and allow students to learn outside of the classroom. The internet and library can provide information for independent study and professional lecturers or articles can be a welcome opportunity for specialist investigation. Each medium is unique and offers its own benefits; furthermore each requires a certain set of skills to be able to take notes from. An interesting classroom will have a combination of all of the above as well as other subject-specific tools for learning. Use medium-term planning to ensure a range of stimuli and offer guidance within each lesson for how to take notes from the medium provided. Below is guidance on how to advise students to take notes from each medium.

Teacher. This is common practice and should be encouraged from the outset of an AS course. Students should be guided through the difference of teacher exposition and class discussion. This can be modelled for them by the teacher making it explicit at the beginning of an exposition that this is teacher explanation and students are expected to take notes. In the beginning students may feel the need to write down their teacher's every word and the students' slow pace can encourage teachers to dictate information rather than explain their subject. Do not dictate; students will simply write without any form of information processing and it only serves to reinforce their belief that you will spoon-feed them knowledge. Structuring the early weeks of notes making will pay dividends in the long term. Consider the following sequence of guidance in taking notes from teacher exposition and how they can be planned for within your subject area in the first few weeks of an AS course.

Week 1: Teacher speaks slowly with regular pauses to allow students to take notes, frequent recap allows students to check and add to their notes with teacher guidance. Teacher does not read, repeat or dictate.

Week 2: Teacher continues to speak slowly but removes the regular pauses to allow students to take notes, frequent recap allows students to check and add to their notes with teacher guidance.

Week 3: Teacher speaks slowly to allow students to take notes. Students check their notes against each other to ensure coverage.

Week 4: Teacher speaks at a regular pace and students check their notes against each other to ensure coverage using a checklist provided by the teacher.

Week 5: Teacher speaks at a regular pace and students individually check their notes using a checklist provided by the teacher to ensure coverage.

Week 6: Teacher speaks at a regular pace and students confidently take notes and ask questions at the end to complete any gaps or areas of confusion. This will become the norm within the classroom.

Book. An 'A' Level teacher's favourite homework activity can be to set students' note taking from the course text book. This is necessary but can be incredibly dull for the student. The teacher can make it livelier by setting mini-challenges for the students. These can include:

◆ a word maximum and minimum;
◆ disallowing connectives;
◆ pre-determined keywords which have to be included;
◆ not allowing notes to exceed one side of A4;
◆ using mapping techniques only;
◆ use of symbols and pictures to highlight keywords and phrases.

If the challenge is varied and an element of competition is introduced students can become more engaged with the activity and more willing to complete their notes ahead of the lesson which can bring enormous benefits to the pace and variety of the lessons. This will be explored further in Chapter Two.

ICT. Whilst the benefits of the information technology revolution to learning are immense, there is a danger of students cutting and pasting downloaded text into their work and gathering information without processing it at any level. If set a research task students can readily access information without reading it or relating it to the wider topics being taught and the specific syllabus requirements. The following suggestions can help a teacher determine whether students have processed downloaded information effectively.

1. Only allow the use of graphic organizer notes when handing in notes taken from the electronic resources.
2. Complete a search of a string of words used by a sample of students to ascertain whether material has been cut and pasted from an easily accessible site.
3. Pair students together for mini-vivas (see Chapter Three) when handing in their notes to determine if the students have processed the notes or simply copied them.
4. Get the students to complete summarizing exercises from their notes prior to handing in to allow the students to show understanding of the notes they have taken.

Summary

Note taking is another vital aspect of an 'A' Level classroom and an essential pre-requisite to advanced learning. Yet it is an area in which students can often be disengaged and learn little from. Move the emphasis from note taking to note making and vary the experience in each lesson. Build discussion of the chosen method of notes into the lesson and raise the importance of the activity through giving each set of notes a direct purpose. If 'A' Level students value their work and are more involved with the gathering of knowledge the greater the understanding and the motivation to learn.

3. Reading

Reading comes as a bit of a shock to many students at AS and A2 level yet can be one of the most pleasurable activities of advanced study. Irrespective of the subject of study, students are required to read specialist subject text in order to inform their subject knowledge as well as encourage enquiry, reasoning and evaluative skills. Reading at GCSE is often based on bite-size pieces of text and suddenly students are expected to read a variety of types of text, long chapters and articles. Many students are expected to complete preparatory reading in advance of their lessons and often do not know where to begin, resulting in wasted time, scanning pages yet taking very little in. Reading longer passages of text or whole articles and chapters requires the same level of planning as the other areas of learning already discussed. As with note taking and discussion a ladder of progression is required in order that the teacher knows where they are aiming for. Inevitably this will vary across subjects; English reading requirements will be far more sophisticated than those of a technology student yet both are of equal importance to the subject area and therefore need to be built into schemes of work. Work with colleagues in planning for progression in reading within your subject area. It may be helpful to enlist the help of a literacy specialist or the librarian who may willingly stock the relevant subject section with your suggested texts. It is a skill that cannot be taken for granted and through a carefully stepped approach and with stimulating choices of text can be truly captivating for both student and teacher. There are many strategies available to help students to interact with the text and engage with the writing on the page. Many of the techniques discussed here may have been addressed through students' literacy or English lessons – it can however be difficult for students to transfer these skills across subjects as well as remembering to use a variety of approaches to reading. The following suggested techniques, well used by my students, will require practice and should be used on a regular basis. Through well-thoughtout teacher planning, techniques can be experimented with through a variety of genre of text depending on the subject and topic of study.

The 'environment' rules discussed in Chapter Five apply to reading as well. Students will benefit from being encouraged to keep an easily erasable pencil at hand for annotation; pen and highlighters can distract the reader when they return to the text, whereas light pencil markings can be helpful to the student whilst easily erased for other readers. Through encouraging students to read around and beyond the pages prescribed by their teacher a more scholarly approach to learning can be encouraged and a student can aim for wider knowledge through independent reading.

A Student guide to reading – stage 1: Skim (for overall impression)

1. Look at titles.
2. Look at headings.
3. Look at summary box.
4. Look at conclusion.
5. Ask questions.

Look at Titles. Before students read the article or chapter skim over the titles to give student a flavour of the focus of the piece student are about to read. This informs student of the direction the text is taking and gives student an indication of length and whether students have prior knowledge of the topic or question.

Look at the Headings. Skimming over the sub-headings will give students a fuller flavour of the text ahead. It will give students a general gist of the nature and argument of the reading and raise any pertinent issues.

Look at the Summary Box. Student text books often have these and so do many articles. They are helpful to students both before and after reading and act as both a taster and reminder of the content and argument of the text.

Look at the Conclusion. This might feel like cheating and reading the last page first but with an academic text, knowing where the final destination is can help steer the reader through often complex text. Do not be tempted to use this stage as a cheat and stop here, this is not enough; it is a starting point.

Ask Questions. What are students expecting to get from the text? This will help keep student reading interactive and not passive. Write these questions down if it helps to focus students and maintain their concentration.

This whole process should only take a few minutes.

Stage 2: Scan (to pick out specific information using key words)

1. Read every fourth word.
2. Linger on subject-specific words.
3. Look for paragraph signposts and link sentences.
4. Read conclusion.

Read Every Fourth Word. It gives students the idea, but not quite. Scanning is about searching for specific information, for example, a key word, name, event, and historian. This will need practice, some people read like this instinctively while others have to labour over every word. By reading every word students are slowing down their reading and not actively using their prior knowledge to support the reading. If this stage is done effectively stage 3 is much easier and more productive.

Linger on Subject-specific Words. Pause on subject-specific words and look them up in another text or dictionary if necessary. If students fail to do this now they may lose their way or take a wrong turn and waste the rest of the reading time.

Focus on Paragraph Signposts and Link Sentences. Effective text will have clearly signposted paragraphs and a conscientious author will have spent a long time determining the order of their paragraphs – just as a student will when constructing an extended written response. They are sometimes known as topic sentences and will follow with explanation and illustrations of the point and conclude with a sentence which links back to the topic. Encourage students to pay attention to these link sentences as they did before for the conclusion; it will help with their understanding of the rest of the paragraph when the reader finally scrutinizes the text.

Read the Conclusion. The student has skimmed this already so knows what it is about in general terms. This time scan it looking for the key words, concepts or themes that have been developed through the rest of the writing.

Stage 3: Scrutinize (selecting and rejecting the relevant text)

1. Read each paragraph.
2. Reread complex text.
3. Pencil key points or queries.

4.   Dwell on key words or argument.
5.   Look back to examine the text in more detail.

Read Each Paragraph. By now the student should be ready to read the whole chapter or article and should feel confident to do so. They already know the direction of each paragraph and need to slow down their reading and take in the content, concepts and development of the argument discussed by the author. Encourage them to go beyond simple location of information and try to interact with the text through their annotation and later through their notes. Students should not be afraid to reject ideas and information and counter the arguments in their own scribblings and thoughts; this is an important aspect of being a student and essential to the classroom debate which will follow the reading.

Reread Complex Text. Some sentences and arguments will require more than one read through and be prepared to reread these parts or asterix them for later reflection.

Pencil Key Points or Queries. Underline the key words and concepts and ask the student to add their own questions and queries for areas that are confusing or contentious – this may have been done in the earlier stages. Through use of virtual learning environments (see Chapter Two) students can discuss these points with each other or pose their thoughts to other students.

Look Back to Examine the Text in More Detail. The final activity should involve careful study of any aspect of the text which requires the reader to pause and needs to be looked back and reflected upon in detail. This may be on the first read or several days later after much thought and further research or further investigation.

Reading in class

Ideally reading should take place in advance of the lesson or as follow up to the lesson but if it is necessary to read in the lesson, experiment with some of the five strategies suggested below:

◆   Disseminated reading – in small groups; each student begins at a different page and then shares their findings with the rest of the group.
◆   Reading agenda – provide a list of specific items (an agenda) students are to look for as they are reading.

◆ Same topic but different genre – offer a range of text to the class which cover the same information but through different genre and compare usefulness of text as well as the content gleaned.

◆ Small group reading – less dull and daunting than reading around the class and allows students time for clarification without the discomfiture of doing so in front of the whole class.

◆ Quiet reading – individual and at a student's own pace but as it is quiet and not silent students can ask questions of each other in relation to the text.

Summary

Reading is a key vehicle to knowledge and analysis in and out of an 'A' Level classroom and an essential requirement to advanced learning. Yet above many other modes of learning it is a life skill, leisure pursuit and due to many factors a growth industry. Many students arrive in their 'A' Level classroom disaffected with reading and unable to meet the literacy challenges expected of them. Reading round the class is a painful process for many and to be avoided at all costs. Using the techniques suggested and others inspired by your literacy experts, reading can be turned to your advantage and be as rewarding as it is informative.

4. Participation

In Section 1 the role of discussion in the classroom and how to encourage students to be involved in classroom talk were considered. This section develops the area of participation and investigates how to get the whole class involved in each and every lesson. Trying to create an inclusive classroom for any age group can be challenging and in post-16 education it can become immensely frustrating as well. Effective participation in classrooms is the chalk face reality of the current national agenda of inclusion is ensuring schools 'include' children from all social, economic and educational spectrums in their provision. DCSF and corresponding government agencies are doing everything they can to create a state system where all students have the same chances as others to develop their potential to the full.

*High achievement is determined by the school's commitment to inclu-
sion and the steps it takes to ensure that every pupil does as well as
possible.*
Handbook for inspecting secondary schools – Ofsted, 2003

Sixth Form centres and colleges are under equal pressure to ensure
students receive an inclusive curriculum through different curriculum opportunities or pathways as they are commonly labelled.
Although this is arguably quite different at AS and A2 level where
entry requirements to sit different courses are set by the college itself,
this remains an important educational point. All students should be
included in the educational provision made available for them. At a
strategic level this is for college leaders and managers to determine
but at a classroom level it is the role of every to teacher to ensure that
all students feel part of the lesson they are attending and have opportunity to confidently participate in the requirements and the demands
of the lesson. This can challenge even the most experienced teacher
and has little to do with the acquisition of subject knowledge.

For a teacher to create a lesson that provides an inclusive environment, a series of planning considerations will be required. The teacher
must be aware of the potential strengths and limitations of the students within the lesson. Furthermore the teacher needs to be clear
of the learning objectives of the lesson and how these can be
achieved by all the students. Additionally the teacher needs an
arsenal of techniques to encourage active participation of all students.
We will assume for the purposes of this section that the teacher is
clear of their lesson objectives, through using methods discussed in
Chapter Three, as well as the students' strengths and weaknesses.
With these provisos in place this section is able to focus on a range
of strategies to encourage the participation of all students in their
learning and create an inclusive lesson, in other words a lesson where
all students are fully involved in the learning and are able to work
towards meeting the lesson objectives and outcomes in an enthusiastic manner.

Getting the whole class involved in the lesson

Class sizes can vary enormously at AS and A2. A Spanish lesson may
have three students whereas a history lesson may have twenty or
more students and vice versa depending on the cohort, tradition of
the subject and the number of specialist teachers available. In a class

of three, it is easier to demand active participation of all students and the lessons may adopt a more tutorial style approach to learning. This cannot work in a larger class and different techniques will need to be employed to ensure all learners are involved in the lesson. A standardized set of teacher notes and lesson plans will not promote or come close to achieving an inclusive classroom; on the contrary the teacher needs to be adaptable to each class and carefully select the appropriate pedagogic methods to ensure all students have the opportunity to be involved. Carefully consider when and with whom the following approaches will work to maximum effect.

Mini Whiteboards. Mini whiteboards are often used as an assessment for learning tool to gauge who has understood a given aspect of the lesson. They encourage all students to respond to a question or idea and enable all students to take part as 'opting out' is not a choice. Each student has his/her own mini whiteboard and dry wipe pen and can use this erasable tool to answer questions as frequently as required. They are non-threatening due to the temporary format of the response the student provides, while they allow the teacher to ensure, at a glance, that all students have provided a response. In a modern foreign language lesson, responses to listening comprehension exercises can be noted, shared and corrected by all students. In a Biology lesson, observations can be noted during a modelled experiment and analysed in practice for students' individual experiments where no redrafting of observations are allowed.

Hand-held Interactive. Handsets offer the same involvement as a mini whiteboard and depending on which software and hardware is employed. It can allow students to go beyond a 'yes/no' response and transfer their answer or idea directly to the whiteboard for further class discussion. If you cannot afford these as a department, the school or college will often be prepared to spend e-learning credits on a set of handsets as long as they are shared across departments and are seen to be actively benefiting learning. A cheaper way to acquire such resources is by contacting the interactive whiteboard providers and offering to pilot or trial their equipment. Most suppliers are developing such equipment and keen to see how they can be used in the classroom.

In source analysis work in a History lesson, handsets allow students to make inferences and send them directly to the whiteboard. The teacher can then sort these and ask for further student responses relating to nature, origin and purpose of the sources being studied. In a mathematics lesson, students can contribute answers after a set period of thinking time and debrief working based on the range of responses.

No Hands Classroom. This is another assessment for learning technique promoted through the National Strategy. The idea is that students do not raise their hands to answer questions; instead the teacher will ask any student at any time to answer a question posed by the teacher or another student. The climate for learning needs to be respectful and non-threatening in order that students, who cannot answer a question they are struggling with, are able to say 'I don't know' without fear of recrimination. It is important to allow students thinking time, a gap of seven to ten seconds from when the question is asked to when the response is solicited. When employing this method, make sure you count the seconds in your head; it is an amazingly long time in a silent classroom. (See Chapter Four – Encouraging Reflective Learners for further discussion.)

Small Group Work. Group work is a popular method of encouraging learners to participate in an activity without the pressure of a large class size or the insecurity of working independently. The size and dynamics of group work play a major role in the level of success for both student and teacher in this type of work and I have experimented with different approaches over several years with all age groups. My research with different groups of GCSE and 'A' Level students over three years in Norfolk schools and colleges, has led me to conclude that the most successful group sizes for more mature learners are not only relatively small, between two and three students, but also most effective when determined by the students rather than imposed by the teacher.

Groups larger than three often result in insufficient involvement by all participants or a sub-divide of the original group into smaller groups thus defeating the original purpose of the group. A group of three forces collaboration between group members; students will have to listen and discuss and in order to reach decisions a majority verdict will have to be debated and in some instances a student will have to concede their line of argument. A group of four or pair can result in deadlock and be divisive for the students involved in both the short term and the long term. A group of three can afford the use of an observer to record work in progress during a sporting activity, field study, experiment or problem-solving activity thus allowing active involvement by the two remaining group members without the worry of noting down proceedings.

By allowing students to chose their co-workers the teacher is offering a degree of trust in the students' choices and helps to support a more harmonious working environment. If the teacher imposes the group dynamics there can be social and personal issues within a group of which the teacher has no knowledge. Such conflict impedes the learning and participation of the group and results in a reduction of motivation and anxiety about issues completely disconnected from the learning objective.

To counter this argument many teachers may argue that students who always choose the same group members they will not experience the benefits and challenges of working with other students. A way of overcoming this problem and allowing students to choose their co-workers but ensuring group dynamics are varied is by determining a set of criteria for group membership. For example, a teacher may wish students to solve a series of mathematical algebraic problems, in order to differentiate the level of challenge the group criteria may be as follows:

◆ all group members must have the same target grade;
◆ one group member must be willing to share their methodology with the rest of the class;
◆ at least two group members must not have worked with each other before.

Consider the dynamics such criteria would determine. Students will be working with similar ability students thus allowing the teacher to set the appropriate level of challenge. The more vocal members of the class will have to be spread across the different groups and similarly the quieter members of the class cannot gather together. Finally the groups will be made up of at least two students who have not previously worked together. The groups will be chosen by the students but be diverse in their composition and make-up. As the teacher gets to know their students better the criteria can be streamlined and be specific to the requirements of the task the group has been formed to undertake. Even better the students can begin to determine their own criteria based on the nature of the task and the skills it requires.

Presentations. Students are regularly asked to give presentations for a variety of reasons. As part of their Key Skills Course post-16 students are required to display a variety of communication skills such as key skills. Key skills are the skills that are commonly needed for success in a range of activities in education and training, work and life in general. QCA define key skills as:

◆ application of number;
◆ communication;
◆ information and communication technology;
◆ improving own learning and performance;
◆ problem solving;
◆ working with others.

The key skills documentation exemplifies standards in all these areas from levels 1–4 with clearly mapped progression. Students will welcome opportunities to demonstrate strategies and progress in these areas and in planning for such occasions more creative approaches to learning can be present in your lessons. As teachers it is possible to build these opportunities into lessons without it appearing to be 'bolted on' to normal classroom practice. Similarly, regular but not over-frequent use of student presentations can help with student participation and involvement in all aspects of the lesson. Not only are effective communication skills a central aspect of student learning, they are also a life skill. Many of the students who frequent AS and A2 classroom will go onto university or to professional jobs which require them to effectively communicate and present their ideas to a range of audience. It is helpful for a student therefore to create a range of presentation opportunities across the school year. Ideally the teacher or department will build progression into these presentation techniques; the key skills coordinator may even provide this framework for a college or Sixth Form. The students themselves would welcome this and it would help their own awareness of the importance of communication styles outside of a specialized subject area. Death by power point is to be avoided as much as possible and through modelling of examples the teacher can show students how to engage an audience and appropriately select the most suitable form of media. An understanding by information and communication technology (ICT) literate students in this field should not be taken for granted. When considering how best to share this skill with students, a teacher is forced to reflect on their own manner of presentation and whether the chosen style of presentation is the most fitting technique to encourage engagement and active participation of their own class.

Prior sections in this chapter have referred to the need for progression in all these areas in order that the teacher and the students know what they are aiming for and more importantly how and with which opportunities they are going to get there. Presentations are no exception to this style of progression planning and Table 1.1 suggests a model of progression for presentations. After consideration of the model, reflect upon the variety of presentation opportunities in your classroom. How might the style and the opportunity operate in your lesson? Presentations can also be linked to independent learning activities as discussed in Chapter Two.

Presentations promote an interesting and varied classroom as well as encouraging all students to participate in the content of the lesson and the way the content is being conveyed and understood. As a key skill and a life skill presenting can be fun, challenging, fulfilling to both student and teacher and an effective tool of participation, as well as meeting the demands of the examination. As with other skills it will require careful management and planning.

Targeting of individual students

The final suggestion for an inclusive classroom is arguably a non-inclusive technique as it is based upon singling out individual students and responding to their needs in order to encourage maximum participation from the targeted student. The goal is that by using this technique as you are just getting to know your class you will get to know your students better and thus promote an inclusive and participatory classroom.

In the early weeks of a teacher–class relationship it can be easy to allow the more dominant individuals to take centre stage and let the quieter students step back. They may or may not be participating in the lesson; can any teacher really judge who is listening and who is always thinking of an answer irrespective of whether they are going to be asked or not? Despite research into active listening techniques is this really possible to do in a class of 20 able 16- and 17-year old students? For some adept and experienced teachers this may be possible but for others a system of targeting students on a random basis will ensure that no student goes unnoticed and 'slips through the net'. The idea is simple; for each lesson the teacher selects two or three students who will be closely monitored throughout the course of the lesson. The teacher then composes a series of questions

Table 1.1 A suggested model of progression for presentation

Presentation style	Presentation opportunities	Minimum requirement	Development stage	Exemplary standard →
Sharing data or information	1. Main part of lesson 2. Whole class or small groups 3. Starter	Giving information using one or two forms of media.	Giving information using a variety of media	Sharing information in a way that engages the audience through selection of relevant media
Supporting/ countering a hypothesis	1. During a debate 2. Conclusion of a series of experiments 3. Plenary	Gives point of view and supports with generalized evidence	Presents prepared information well and tries to respond to comments and questions	Confidently defends own argument through well-chosen evidence and counters opposition in a calm and well-reasoned manner
Speaking on a topic to an unknown audience	1. Open evening 2. Celebration event 3. Invited audience 4. Virtual audience	Gives information which is understood by the audience	Considers audience in selection of information and method of presentation	Communicates in a clear and confident manner using information relevant to the audience

or a checklist to monitor the level of involvement the student is demonstrating within the lesson. These questions could include:

◆ Are they participating in class discussion?
◆ Are they quick on task?
◆ Have they completed their preparation work and homework?
◆ Are they involved in group work by putting forward ideas and listening to group members' discussion?

Without the students' knowledge the teacher keeps a simple log or tally chart of the targeted students' involvements throughout the lesson and action can be taken based on the findings. For example, the student may score highly on participation on discussion but may fair less well in group work. To develop the students' participation in group work, some of the group work techniques discussed previously may need to be employed. Conversely a student who refuses to talk in class discussion but is much happier in a small group may need to work through some of the active talk strategies (also discussed previously). A teacher may argue that they do this every lesson with all students; in reply I would ask that teacher to reflect how far they plan each lesson based on the needs of all their students to create a truly inclusive classroom. Observing a non-participating student is the first part; planning to develop the level of participation of each student is the challenge.

Summary

Participation in an 'A' Level classroom is a true sign of a captivated class and an essential requirement to advanced learning. When managed well, it creates an equitable, confident and intellectually challenging learning environment where all students will be working towards achieving the objectives of the lesson. This is a highly desirable position for any teacher to be in and one the teacher should constantly strive for. The future success of your 'A' Level students in their exam and in life depends on their involvement in your lessons. With a positive environment and reciprocated respect students will want to participate in your lessons and become better learners as a consequence of it. OfSTED referred to an outstanding

> lesson at a Birmingham Sixth Form College as demonstrating that 'learners participate effectively in class discussions and respond well to teachers' questions'.

5. Games

I like it when you introduce a bit of competition Miss! I like winning.
Fraser, 17 years old

I like it when we play those games, there is an element of surprise and you never quite know what will happen next.
Rebecca, 17 years old

Anything with a sticky note, you know you are going to have to think!
Vicky, 17 years old

At the end of each AS and A2 course I asked my students to feedback on their 'A' Level classroom experiences. I ask them to discuss lessons they had found challenging, lessons they had found fun and lessons they believe they had learned in. Their answers are surprisingly similar and the quotes above reflect the general consensus of most groups. They enjoy games and activities which deviated from the normal classroom practice, the lessons they enjoyed engaged them and consequently they felt they learned more. The challenge comes through the complexity or surprise within the game itself. Most Year 12s are around 16 years of age and when a Year 12 student begins their AS course it is important to remember they little older than when they left your Year 11 classroom a few months earlier. They have not metamorphosized over the summer into erudite academics and it is important to remember this when planning lessons. College or Sixth Form should be a place of learning but surely we want them to enjoy their learning experience and injecting some fun or competition into lessons should add to and enhance their learning experience. This is not to suggest our Year 12/13 classrooms should degenerate into entertainment zones of endless electronic interactivity and party games; instead we can use ideas from parlour games and their modern equivalents to keep students challenged, captivated and a little bit nervous about what will happen next.

Sticky notes

Every teacher should have at least one pack of sticky notes in their pencil case. They can be used for quick fire starter activities or a consolidation plenary, either way they usually raise a smile. Below are ten suggestions of activities to do with a sticky note.

1. *Guess who*: Write words, phrases or names of people, places or topics studied on the sticky note, stick it to a student's forehead and the rest of the group have to guess-who (or what) it is using a set number of questions. These can be individuals who make up a history, music or psychology syllabus or more abstract mathematical theories and computer terminology.

2. *Secret identities*: Guess-who in reverse; hand each student a secret identity as they enter the classroom, known only to the student who has the sticky note, the rest of the class have to determine who or what the student is based on a series of questions or through clues revealed during the course of the lesson. Again this can be applied to theories, formulas and terminology.

3. *Homework check*: Write three ideas or comments from homework on the sticky note and stick on the wall for later checking.

4. *Homework feedback*: Students write down any anxieties or questions they have about the homework in order that the teacher can address them in a discreet way.

5. *First to 3/5/10 . . .*: Each student has to write the chosen number of pieces of information they learned in the prior lesson on the sticky note and stick it on the board.

6. *Questions*: Each student writes down a question they have about the topic of the lesson, use for the plenary to check all questions have been answered.

7. *Questions*: As above but hand out the questions to the students and ask the students to answer each other's questions as part of the plenary.

8. *Guess the lesson objective*: Part way through the lesson, ask the students to write on their sticky what they think the lesson objective is; reveal the objective only when

absolutely necessary. This may even be as late as the plenary. It is not compulsory to reveal lesson objectives at the start of the lesson. They are essential to planning and should be shared at the appropriate moment in the lesson.

9. *Memory test*: Condense reading or notes on to a sticky note and use only the sticky to answer a question in test conditions.

10. *Speech*: Students give a presentation using only a sticky note as a prompt.

All these suggestions will make up a small part of a bigger lesson but they will keep the lesson varied, provide it with pace and help smooth sometimes difficult transition phases of lessons. Experiment with a few and use regularly but not frequently as any game played too often can quickly become dull.

Role play

Highly popular with history and modern foreign language teachers alike, role play forms a common part of an 11–14 teaching diet but seems to fade out in post-16 teaching. In discussion with teachers who chose not to use role play with AS and A2 students, they cited lack of time, unwillingness of students to take part due to their age, inappropriate sense of frivolity and lack of academic rigour as the main reasons for not using role play in 'A' Level classrooms. The value of role play lies in the students' ability to take on a different persona and follow an event, make decisions or re-evaluate prior judgements in character. This is challenging at any level and if the student is forced to think outside of their own immediate viewpoint the level of thinking is more than appropriate for an 'A' Level student. Students will be required to research their character and consider the influences that will affect their judgements and interpretations of events. This will encourage engagement with a knowledge base as well as more rigorous understanding of the impact of events or theories on 'real' people. In my experience I have rarely met a group who oppose role play though some have needed more encouragement than others. Role play can be based on abstracts as well as people and simply requires a little creativity. Examples for different subject areas are suggested below.

◆ A Geography lesson can recreate a council meeting to discuss how to manage the development of the local coastal area.
◆ Psychology students may use the classroom as a working controlled experiment with students taking character roles as the psychologist, the observer and the observed.
◆ A government crisis meeting can be held in an Economics lesson to discuss a situation of market failure and whether the government should intervene and if so, to what extent.
◆ A chemical spill has taken place at a chemical plant nearby. In a Mathematics lesson mathematicians have been summoned to calculate how soon the nearby residences will need to be evacuated given the container dimensions, the chemical spillage rate, the location of the residential district and other necessary data. Demands from the local services for a response can add pressure to the proceedings.

Summary

Which lesson is a student more likely to remember? Taking notes from their teacher and answering questions on a sheet about global warming or attending a global warming conference to discuss carbon foot prints as a representative of an invited country. Now ask the following question: which lesson are you more likely to remember? If you want to truly captivate your class you will need to be captivating and through creative approaches to teaching your AS and A2 students will be counting the days to their next lesson with you. Not only will they enjoy the tasks you devise but their engagement with the activity will improve their creative thinking, help them to learn and motivate them independently. Make sure time is allocated for consolidation activities to reinforce the learning.

6. Writing

Writing is a hugely contentious topic of academic debate. The media regularly send out messages that the next generation of adolescents are illiterate and cannot spell without a word spell checker. Enter newspaper quote on failing literacy rates. When Tony Blair repeated 'Education, education, education!' to his voting public was he really referring to 'Literacy, literacy, literacy'? Vast research has taken place in seeking to discover how to make our children literate and the National Literacy Strategy has invested time, money and resources into seeking to raise the literacy standards of all our children since the turn of the century. Writing remains the key means for monitoring, measuring and assessing pupil progress and understanding. Furthermore all 'A' Level students are examined through writing. There are some examinations which take a practical form, for example, in subjects such as Physical Education and Art but they also have written papers to complete as well. In addition to this, teachers expect their students to keep a written confirmation of their learning through notes, charts, tables and other recording tools. In other words, writing is a necessary and important requisite of AS and A2 students' learning in a formative and summative sense.

All teachers are responsible for developing the literacy needs of their students and while some students enjoy the challenge of writing, other students find it tedious, onerous and a chore. This can lead to and be the result of a vast range of literacy competency within any 'A' Level classroom and for a non-literacy specialist this can appear overwhelming. This section will not offer theoretical discussion on the merits and demerits of approaches to teaching literacy; instead it will offer strategies to engage and motivate your students in written work and support their written outcomes. These are broken into two areas, with three broad suggestions for each.

◆ How can the writing be intrinsically interesting?
◆ How can the writing be supported?

How can the writing be intrinsically interesting?

Vary the Audience. Encourage students to write for an audience other than you or the examiner. This is explored further in Chapter Four. Possible examples are teacher, examiner, parent, friend, grandparent, younger child, GCSE student or an academic.

Write in Different Genre. Again this varies the style of writing and encourages students to study a range of genre. It is helpful for the teacher to model examples of different genre and highlight the key features of different texts. Possible examples are a school book, exam, magazine or journal, news article, information guide or a set of instructions. The National Strategy offers an array of exemplar materials in this area.

Creative Outcomes for Writing. Students can give a sense of purpose to their work by writing for a real audience. Outside agencies are often pleased to receive students' work and will offer feedback to students if possible.

Examples of a real audience include other staff, parents, open evening literature, magazines and journals, newspaper, local resource centre, university and other students.

How can the writing be supported?

Scaffolds. Scaffold are discussed in detail in Chapter Two. The main purpose of a scaffold is to offer an agreed level of support and guidance such as a writing frame; in line with the students' progress the scaffold can be dismantled and eventually withdrawn.

Criteria. This is discussed in detail in Chapter Three and is an important aspect of assessment for learning to clarify the foci and expectation of a piece of work.

Model. Another product of the National Strategy and commonly used in classrooms across the country. Modelling encourages the teacher to demonstrate a style or method or learning or outcome. In literacy terms this can be tremendously helpful to an insecure student and provide and initial framework for their written work. At AS and A2 level overuse of modelling can limit individuality and lead to formulaic responses.

Summary

Writing is the means by which 'A' Level students are summatively assessed and students will require guidance in formal examination writing. This is explored in Chapter Three. During their year of study however it is useful to offer students a range of writing opportunities to explore genre and audience.

Using these techniques can motivate and discipline students as writers and allow them to explore a range of texts whilst developing their subject knowledge. Build subject-specific assessment objectives into the written task to ensure subject rigour remains intact

Chapter summary

Enlivening strategies are not designed to make the classroom a 'fun' place to be for the purpose of entertaining students. The techniques and strategies suggested are ways of developing the students' ability to learn and engage with their subject. Consider which strategies may work most effectively at the start of a course and which require greater progress through the course before they can be introduced. Activities work most effectively if they are revisited, however too much of the same can become tedious and the classroom will stagnate again. Be prepared for resistance from staff and students; staff may feel threatened and passive learning requires less effort from students. Also be prepared to work outside of your own 'comfort zone' and challenge your own practice through new and different approaches to teaching and learning within the classroom. Finally allow time to reflect upon successes and failures and seek advice where necessary.

2 | Creating independent students

With a little help and structure I could work independently. Most lessons were started with a basic idea or concept and we built upon it ourselves.

Becky, Year 12

The pressures of an end of course examination can create a pedagogic straight-jacket for teachers. Consider for a moment a secondary school teacher who prides himself on his creativity and ability to encourage students to explore the subject through a range of learning styles and research tools. This teacher wishes to employ such an approach to learning at AS and A2 but feels under immense pressure from the Head of Sixth Form to get a minimum A–C and A–E grade pass rate as well as adding 'value' to the students minimum target grade. The teacher begins to make less use of his creative approaches to learning and moves towards a more didactic style of teaching in order to ensure that the students have the correct body of knowledge to be secure in the examination. Lessons become content driven and lesson objectives are focused around the specification content rather than the necessary concepts and skills which enable the learner to become a disciplined student of their subject. Over time this becomes the normal mode of lesson delivery and the students become accustomed to the teacher 'spoon-feeding' them the content. Application, evaluation and synthesis of the content take place as homework activities and are rarely discussed in class. The well-intentioned teacher loses sight of the creativity he originally aimed for and the students become passive and teacher-dependent learners.

This sequence may at first sight appear extreme but how common a picture does it paint of teachers in 'A' Level classrooms across the country? How often do lesson plans become driven by content in AS and A2 classrooms rather than by concepts or processes, in order to meet the requirements of the specification and allow both the teacher and student to be assured that the exam content has been covered. The teacher is well-intentioned and results will most likely be in line with target grades but consider what is happening to the students' development as learners during this process. Their dependency on the teacher restricts their ability to act and think independently about their subject and their learning. Consequently the students look to the teacher as a deliverer of knowledge instead of a facilitator of their learning.

This chapter focuses on the area of independent learning, initially through discussion of some of the varying interpretations of what independent learning really means. The chapter will then give consideration to a series of more interesting and innovative strategies to develop students as self-determining and self-directed learners. As in Chapter One, some of the techniques will be familiar to you in 11–16 teaching and are discussed in theoretical and practical terms and exemplified through subject examples.

7. Independent learning and its importance

Have you ever sat with your colleagues in a department meeting and asked the question: 'What do you want 'A' Level students to be able to do and to have achieved by the end of their course?'

I regularly use this question as an ice-breaker for 'A' Level teacher-training workshops and unsurprisingly the responses are often similar. The top ten responses are (in no particular order).

1. be confident individuals;
2. capable of making up their own mind;
3. able and wanting to discuss the subject with their teacher and peers;
4. enthusiastic about the subject;
5. an effective communicator;
6. self-evaluative;
7. an independent learner;
8. get a good grade;
9. equipped with skills for life;
10. open minded.

This is a commendable list and each is a highly desirable quality in any young adult. Yet the measurable quality of achievement is one statement within a much less tangible list. Teachers clearly believe good grades are important but most place it within a wider context of a successful and responsible learner. Furthermore many teachers readily acknowledge that if the other qualities are in place, students will be able to meet or exceed their target grades. All this suggests that many teachers wish to educate young people in a wide-reaching sense of the term yet due to a result-driven environment they can lose sight of it in their day-to-day planning.

The 'cage' built around learning as a result of the league table culture often begins much earlier than post-16 education. KS2 and 3 tests, followed by GCSE can create a culture of teacher dependency that limits the opportunities for students to develop skills of independence and more specifically independent learning.

The National Curriculum implemented from 2008 is trying to address this issue with pupils now receiving a statutory entitlement to personal, learning and thinking skills. This is categorized into six aspects of learning which are as follows:

◆ self-manager;
◆ creative thinker;
◆ independent learner;
◆ team worker;
◆ reflective learner;
◆ communicator.

These bear a striking resemblance to the earlier teachers' list and represent the national trend to move away from an examination straight-jacket towards a reflective approach to learning with an understanding by teachers and pupils that successful learning is about more than just achieving high grades. This concept of independent learning is not new but it has become buried within the existing examination driven education system and it is the responsibility of teachers to liberate it and develop the capacity of our students to think and act as independent learners.

To ask a group of teachers what independent learning means is a controversial question. Some regard it as working by themselves, others regard it as understanding how to learn by themselves and many regard it as possessing the capacity to set and answer questions through their own direction. There is a large quantity of academic writing and discourse as to what an independent learner looks like and references for further discussion are provided in the reference section of the book. The question should ideally be addressed by you as the teacher and by your colleagues. Whatever the definition, it needs to be a coherent one for the student and they need to understand the definition in order to be able to work towards it. As a department or other group of professionals, it is worth trying to agree a continuum of independence which recognizes the interactive and interdependent nature of independent learning as well as the need for self-reliance. This continuum can reflect the minimum requirement of an independent learner to the most you could reasonably expect an A2 student to be able to achieve. The aim of each department member is to move students along the continuum at their own pace. What remains of key importance is the professional dialogue and research which supports this departmental conversation.

Summary

Independent learning is a learning tool and a life skill and it is a disservice to AS and A2 students, to not strive to develop it. Its ambiguity as a term can lead to confusion and misrepresentation by teachers and therefore in student understanding. Discuss as a department which areas of independence you value and if possible increase departmental expertise in this field through academic study or engaging in action research. Map opportunities for independent learning across the curriculum and begin at the start of the AS course.

8. Developing independence from the beginning

Teaching 'independence' appears to be a paradox. If a teacher provides a structure for learning, by definition they are removing an element of independent study yet if a teacher leaves a student to survive autonomously, the teacher is negating their responsibility to enable the student to learn. Independent learning is open to interpretation depending on the level of independence a teacher wishes to instil in his/her students. The contradiction can become less complex if the teacher determines that their learning objective is for a student to govern and accomplish their studies in an autonomous manner. Independent learning in other words is the goal not the starting point.

This is a commendable objective especially if it is intended for post-16 students who will be expected to work independently in a higher education institution or prospective employment. To not equip students with such skills is a grave disservice to their future ability to engage in independent action and thought. However, while this is an admirable learning objective it can be regarded as being rather trite and requires greater consideration and analysis.

Reconsider our original question: 'What do you want 'A' Level students to be able to do and to have achieved by the end of their course?' If this is now determined and independent learning is an important aspect of your answer, a further question is raised: 'How are you going to get students to this point by the end of the course?'

Knowing how to get students to this end point becomes a crucial part of short, medium and long-term planning and most importantly planning for progression. It requires a teacher to look beyond their immediate course of study and at the big picture of AS and A2 and where learning opportunities fit together. It can be argued that knowing where you want students to be by the age of 18 or 19 requires retrospective planning as far back as their entry into secondary school at age 11. Providing coherence to the curriculum necessitates progression mapping across three key stages from ages 11–19.

Table 2.1 offers a suggested model of progression for independent learning and addresses the characteristics independent learning might display at three different levels within three different contexts. Each of these areas is designed to encourage a student to autonomously engage in their studies and to think by themselves, albeit with limited intervention. Some students will master such techniques very quickly, readily show a preference for this method of working and operate almost immediately at exemplary level. Other students may need to attempt each area of independent learning in isolation with the reassurance of a teacher or mentor to support their learning journey. With the necessary guidance the student will achieve a breakthrough in their learning and become equipped to set, solve, or present a task through self-determining means. A final few will continue to struggle with the whole process of working independently and continually seek instruction in all aspects of their studies from their teacher. As with all areas of 'A' Level study there will be immense differentiation within a class of post-16 students and a

Table 2.1 A suggested model of progression for independent learning

Area of independent learning	Opportunities	Minimum requirement	Development stage	Exemplary standard →
Setting a problem	1. Questioning 2. Setting an hypothesis	Can choose from a selection of questions or given hypotheses the one they would like to study the most	Can formulate own questions and hypothesis based on prior study and knowledge	Can formulate different types of questions and hypothesis to address conceptual or skills focus of study
Solving the problem	1. Research methodology 2. Recording the findings 3. Identifying gaps	Can use a range of resources/media to research and note taking skills to record findings	Can select the most appropriate method of research and recording techniques to research and record findings	Will identify strengths and limitations of different recording and research methods based on nature of the task
Presenting the solution	1. Identifying audience 2. Choosing form of media 3. Next steps for learning	Can vary style of presentation based on nature of audience	Can plan and create a presentation most appropriate in style and content to identified audience	Can select content of presentation based on intended audience and identify gaps in learning based upon this

range of teaching strategies will need to be gradually introduced to promote autonomy in learning. Invariably many of these approaches to learning would be of greater benefit if introduced much earlier into the educational process and were viewed as routine to students. Unfortunately, the pressures of examination statistics result in teachers becoming reluctant to allocate time to the process of teaching independent learning. The fear of a students failure to complete an aspect of their AS or A2 course is regarded as simply to great a risk and as previously discussed teachers revert to 'spoon-feeding techniques'. This in turn leads to students missing out on opportunities to experience and develop an understanding of how to organize and execute their own learning. By the time students reach an 'A' Level classroom, expectations and perceptions of a teacher's role are fixed. Students share an unwillingness to operate independently of their subject teacher who they regard as the supplier of subject knowledge and examination specification.

It may appear futile to move to a new approach to learning so late in a students educational development but with a carefully managed transition from GCSE to AS and later to A2, clear expectations can be shared with students thus removing any preconceived misconceptions by students and teachers of each other's role in the classroom. Transfer can be more informed in a high school Sixth Form than in a further education college, however in both cases the teacher and students will benefit from using techniques from Chapter Three to identify the level of prior learning and experience in all areas of subject knowledge and learning skills. As with all learning intentions, the level of teacher support and autonomy a teacher expects is of greater benefit when shared explicitly with students from the very outset of a course. By sharing the intention to encourage student independence a teacher is recognizing that he is not simply expecting students to be able to operate through their own actions; on the contrary the teacher is clarifying that he will guide them through this process and turn them into successful students who know how to learn rather than students who can only pass their chosen exam. Arguably independent learning will challenge a teacher's determination and belief more than any other area of AS or A2 study. A teacher has to believe in the short-, medium- and long-term value of developing the ability and capability to complete their course with skills that go far beyond those measured by external examiners.

Summary

Independent learning requires more than token gestures to 'working by oneself'. It requires planning, structure and guidance across a taught course and clearly identified progression based on the changing cohort of students. Future learners who are beneficiaries of the 2008 National Curriculum may be far more adept at independent learning than the current generation and models of progression will need constant re-evaluation. Agreed and share routes of progression crystallize teachers' thinking and understanding in this area of learning and will require informed and articulated teachers' debate before being accessed to students. Be prepared for students to struggle and fail in the short term but through informed reflection and guidance the majority will succeed in the long term.

9. Providing the scaffolds for independent learning

The term scaffolding is regularly used in literacy based subjects where a support is offered to students, often on an examination paper, to help structure their answer and offer suggestions of information to include in a response. At GCSE many students value the support the scaffold can offer and find its absence in an AS or A2 exam nerve wracking and even isolating. In this section the term scaffolding is used in the context of a technique designed to support a students transition into AS or A2 study and assist their progress in becoming independent learners. As a student becomes more adept in a given area of their study, the scaffold can be gradually withdrawn and packed away for use at a later date if support is temporarily required. Four areas in your students' teaching diet are desirable as independently driven activities and may require scaffolding in their early stages. They are reading, note-taking and researching which are considered below. Homework and time management are referred to in Section 10.

Reading

Reading comes as a shock to many students at AS and A2 level, yet it is necessary and of immense value and for some, highly pleasurable.

GCSE is full of bite size pieces of text and suddenly student are expected to read a variety of types of text, long chapters and articles. Many students are expected to complete preparatory reading in advance of their lessons and often do not know where to begin, resulting in wasted time turning pages, yet taking very little in. As a teacher it is important to help students interact with the text and engage with the writing on the page.

Many of the techniques discussed below are based on ideas from the National Strategy and will have been addressed through student's Literacy or English lessons – some students can find it immensely difficult to transfer these skills across subjects and may need to be reminded, prompted or taught from scratch. The following techniques will require initial teaching, frequent practice and for maximum impact should be used on a regular basis both in and out of class. Advising students to purchase the tools of the trade may seem infantile but will be of benefit to teacher and student in the short and long term. These tools include:

◆ an easily erasable pencil which should be used for annotation; light pencil markings can be helpful to a student whilst easily erased for other readers;
◆ Pen and highlighters to embolden photocopied resources, directing students to key aspects of the text.

Students will struggle to read anything beyond a text book or prescribed reading in the first few weeks and two strategies will help in this. First, publish a reading list for the term ahead with relevant text book chapters, articles and library books. This will encourage a more mature approach to learning where you are simply expecting the student to do this. There are no excuses for not completing the reading and as the teacher you make it clear from the start that excuses will not be tolerated. If students fail to complete their preparatory reading exclude them from the lesson; this will not be well received and I am yet to meet a re-offender after such exclusion. This need not be a removal from class more of a physical segregation; it often has greater impact if the student actually witnesses the task the others students are engaged in and is made aware of the activities they are missing out on. This can work especially well if the lesson is dynamic and interesting and it is visible that a lack of subject knowledge would impede the students progress in that lesson.

Make it clear that a student who is not prepared for their learning cannot learn and it is therefore not acceptable to expect everyone else to be held back by one students inefficiency. Some would think that this is too harsh, but if students are expected to be independent learners they must accept consequences for failing to behave responsibly. Remember to encourage students to read around and beyond the prescribed pages as you will be recommending the minimum requirement and students should aim for wider knowledge through independent reading. The sequence set out below offers a guide to AS reading and is discussed in full in Chapter One.

How to read

Stage 1: Skim (for overall impression)

1. Look at titles.
2. Look at headings.
3. Look at summary box.
4. Look at conclusion.

Stage 2: Scan (to pick out specific information using key words)

1. Read every fourth word.
2. Linger on subject-specific words.
3. Look for paragraph signposts and link sentences.
4. Read conclusion.

Stage 3: Scrutinize (selecting and rejecting the relevant text)

1. Read each paragraph.
2. Reread complex text.
3. Pencil key points or queries.
4. Dwell on key words or argument.
5. Look back to examine the text in more detail.

Note taking

Effective teaching of note taking skills as discussed in Chapter One will liberate a student's ability to act and research independently, especially if taught from the very beginning of the AS course. Note taking in itself is arguably not an independent activity in meta-cognitive terms yet once a student is self-determining the purpose of their notes and the style in which they should be taken, a student is beginning to operate and make decisions free of your direction and guidance and is thus becoming a truly independent learner.

Research

Often viewed by students as the 'get on with it on your own' part of AS and A2 study it is one of the solitary pursuits of post-16 study. This does not mean that individual research equates to independent learning. Is the information gatherer learning or simply 'doing'? How can a post-16 student become an effective researcher? Research assistants are a valued commodity in many areas of adult employment and their role requires training and expertise. Teachers therefore need to equip their students with the tools of research and help them to use their research time efficiently and without risk of future plagiarism. As with the previously mentioned skills areas, guide students through their first experiences of research and plan for a gradual personalized withdrawal of support. Below are a list of strategies you can use with students to support their development as independent researchers.

♦ Introduce students to a range of research resources and data in class to raise their awareness of possible research avenues.
♦ Ask students to contribute to whole class research on a regular basis to establish a culture of shared learning.
♦ Create a class research board or use the virtual learning environment (VLE) (Section 12) to share research findings.
♦ Insist all individually produced work has a minimum of one piece of information that cannot be derived from whole class work or texts.
♦ Use the reading techniques with a range of research data and resources.
♦ Encourage field research whenever possible.
♦ Visit libraries (even the college library) and research facilities together and make use of resident experts.
♦ Use video conferencing for online research at nationally based sites (e.g. National Archive).
♦ Show an interest in the students individual discoveries.
♦ Invite a local researcher (Media, University, Council) to visit your school or college and inform students how they work.

Summary

Reading, research and note taking are basic tools of AS and A2 learning yet is easy to make assumptions regarding students' level of competency in these areas. Students cannot embark upon independent learning without a basic skill set to help them through. It is worth spending most of the first half term of an AS course introducing, developing and consolidating these basics. Each learner will be at a different development stage and it is worth undertaking some diagnostic work in the first few weeks of a course to gauge the capability of each student in these areas and plan accordingly. Six weeks of ground work at the start of the course will pay long-term dividends for all involved.

10. Study outside of the classroom

Use of study time

Students of AS and A2 are required to complete a large amount of work outside of the classroom. Time is allocated to them within their timetables to do so and is often labelled as one of the following: study period, self-directed time, private study, preparation time or other college-specific phrase. Each label has an expectation that allocated time will be self-directed and autonomous in nature. A teacher will most probably set the task required for this private study time but the allocated time management and the means by which the task is completed will largely be determined by the student.

The method by which this time is directed, used and reflected upon will impact on a student's ability to become an independent learner. A student's capacity to be able to learn on their own can be maximized through effective co-planning of this time by both teacher and student. Below are 10 points worthy of consideration in your planning of out of classroom study to help a student make improved use of their self-directed study time.

(a) Set tasks for study time together for the first few weeks of a course.

(b) Set tasks a student must complete on their own to develop autonomy.

(c) Set tasks a student must complete within a small group to develop self-direction.

(d) Vary the tasks set within a given time frame to maintain motivation.

(e) Make use of tasks set within lessons to ensure each task has purpose.

(f) Ask the student to keep a time-log to develop time management skills.

(g) Return to similar tasks to ensure progression in these areas.

(h) Acknowledge work completed to maintain motivation.

(i) Discuss method of working and levels of independence within each task with each student or as a class.

(j) Make time for reflection of study time in and out of the classroom.

What do all these mean in practical terms for a post-16 student?

Independent study is arguably both 'a learning activity and a capacity to be developed' (Michelle O'Doherty *Learn Higher*) There now follow two series of suggested strategies that aim to do just this; the first deals with independent learning activities and the second with developing the capacity to learn independently.

To clarify the difference between the two the former deals with activities a student undertakes independent of the teacher to demonstrate their autonomy and ability to operate without the structured direction and involvement of the teacher. The second considers the processes a student undertakes to advance their understanding of their own independent learning and how to 'take the initiative, with or without the help of others, in diagnosing the learning needs, formulating learning goals, identifying human and material resources for learning, choosing and implementing appropriate learning strategies, and evaluating outcomes' [Knowles (1975)].

Independent learning activities

1. *Preparatory reading for use in class*: For General Studies publish a half termly reading list using a range of newspaper articles,

web sites and core text. The reading must be completed in advance of the lesson and the teacher must keep to the intended schedule or the value of reading will be reduced.

2. *Select own reading via a reading list or use of search facilities to enhance understanding*: To complement the published reading list ask students to research and add another title to the list, the student will need to summarize the title and offer a critique on how it can extend student knowledge and understanding.

3. *Selecting a question from a suggested list*: When studying business functions as part of the Business Studies AS syllabus, student selects a question to investigate and prepares a response to with a case study example from a range of questions relating to the marketing function.

4. *Formulating own question within a suggested framework*: Using model questions from a suggested AS list, ask A2 students to formulate their own question for investigation, direct their focus to an area of interest or difficulty to either motivate or challenge.

5. *Selecting an outcome for learning from a suggested list*: Create a list of creative and real outcomes for student work and ask students to choose the outcome for their work; this can take a written or non-written form. For example, geographical field study could be presented as a tourism marketing pitch, geographical association article, movie-maker file, podcast.

6. *Formulating own outcome for learning based on intended audience*: Psychology students are expected to become familiar with techniques for analysing and collecting data; encourage their final report to be presented in an outcome of their choosing based on range of audiences. For example, lecturers, patients, government agency or novices.

7. *Preparing a starter activity for whole class use*: These can be shared out at the start of a half term to coordinate with the reading list. The students need to be aware that a starter engages the students in the topic and is not designed to reveal too much knowledge.

8. *Small research based projects for feedback to whole class*: Presentations can be dull and audience learning limited and it is advisable to use these with caution and spread them out over the course of a year. A2 Government and politics expects students to be paying 'close attention to world events via relevant media' OCR. This is an ideal opportunity for a research based projects, designed to connect real events to the taught course and can be interesting to research as well as informative for the audience.

9. *Devising revision guidance for use within whole class structure*: A Norfolk school created its own revision DVD which was subsequently marketed to local schools. The whole class was onboard with the project and results reflected the student motivation.
10. *Sharing findings with a person other than the teacher*: Local companies, educational establishments and media organizations are often intrigued and fascinated by the work of post-16 students. A local business may find local business studies research of practical use; in the same way the local council can make use of home economic, resources management surveys. Encourage students to share their findings beyond the classroom through college communication e-shots or actively seeking an interested audience.

Learning independently

1. Keep a learning log to monitor use of time and nature of study outside of the classroom.
2. Make use of scaffolds and support to begin with but remove such structures at own pace not as directed by the teacher.
3. Self-determine when there is a need to return to scaffolds and structures for support.
4. Action plan for learning through use of a work plan or schedule.
5. Identify own routes of research and support.
6. Seek peer assessment and feedback to improve work further.
7. Self-reflect upon areas of strength and set targets for future improvement.
8. Employ efficient use of study time and recognize when rest time is needed.
9. Share findings.
10. Be prepared to ask for help.

Time Management. This is a challenging to all learners irrespective of age and requires discipline, practice and ultimately experience. Post-16 students will require support and advice in how to manage the balance the many facets of their busy academic, social and home lives. There will be pressure on individual students beyond our immediate understanding and teachers need to be respectful of the demands placed upon students outside of our subject remit and expectations. Helping students plan their busy week often falls into the remit of the personal tutor or college director and the subject teacher can only play a small role in helping the student to plan their time effectively. Student diaries and work schedules can help with big picture planning but at a subject level there are strategies to support a student through their working week. A useful set of time management strategies are suggested below.

1. Give minimum and maximum time allocations to assignments.
2. Provide a time sheet for an extended task to help students coordinate their time planning.
3. Make use of fixed time allowances for in class activities to prevent over and under use of time allocation.
4. Do not create time pressures through unrealistic deadlines such as the next day.
5. Publish reading, research and assignment deadlines in advance to help a student coordinate their work schedule.
6. Agree interim deadlines to prevent later catastrophe.
7. Deal with late submissions sensitively but firmly.
8. Exclude students from in class activities if they have not completed the necessary preparation work.
9. Group work can help students understand the importance of time management when working as a team.
10. Build reflection time into lessons to address the use of time management.

Summary

In conclusion the teacher can support independent learning and plan for personalized withdrawal of scaffolds throughout the period of AS and A2 study. A student cannot be expected to work without such intervention or guidance and greater long-term damage will be done to a student's engagement with their own learning if such structures are not planned for. To create an independent learner requires a range of guided activities and allocated time or reflection of the learning process in order that the student can evaluate their own approach to learning and their involvement with it. Learning is not a solitary activity – it is inter-dependent on social, environmental and psychological factors and a student's level of co-dependence will vary with the individual and accordingly planning for this should be as personalized as possible.

11. Models for independent learning

The previous sections suggest that effective independent learning is, perhaps, too often engendered by teacher-directed structure. To assist in the process of *self*-directed learning, a model or initial framework can provide the necessary structure to prompt student thinking and planning. Furthermore such a framework can emphasize the importance of self-review and self-evaluation of student's own work thus developing the level of autonomy even further. Various independent learning models have been developed with the intention of 'facilitating, self-directed, reflective and critical learning on the part of individual learners,' (Jarvis 2003) but research offers very little evidence that any model has undergone sustained use at post-16 level.

One of the most commonly used independent learning frameworks is designed by Belle Wallace and is known as the TASC Framework (TASC is an acronym for Thinking Actively in a Social Context). This Framework is designed to 'accommodate all learners and to be a universal framework that would allow and encourage differentiation'. (Wallace 2007). The TASC Wheel represents a universal cycle for developing an 'expert' problem-solving process and encourages learners to begin their task or study by considering what they already know and to 'gather and organize' their existing knowledge in relation to the task or topic. Learners then 'identify' the task and interrogate what is being asked of them; this is then followed by generation of ideas in relation to the task in hand and concludes with a decision on which idea is the best. Once a decision has been made learners begin the task by entering the 'implementing' part of the TASC Wheel with the motivational phrase 'Let's do it!' Thereafter follows an evaluation and subsequently a communication phase where learners question how well they are doing and share their work with an audience of choice. The TASC Framework concludes with the question

'What have I learned?' in the 'Learn from Experience' segment of the Wheel.

Belle Wallace maintains that the segments of the TASC Wheel take varying amounts of time and need not be followed in a linear fashion as learners often fluctuate between each part of the Wheel. Learners will determine their journey around the Wheel based on their individual progress and self-reflection, and also after discussion with their peers or their teacher.

It is important to state here that the TASC Wheel is underpinned by a broad network of Basic Thinking Skills, Advanced Thinking Skills and Tools and Strategies for Learning. (See Wallace and Maker 2004 for details of the full TASC structure.)

Teachers may have come into contact with the TASC Framework as a tool for teaching more-able learners and the National Association for Able Children in Education (NACE) support TASC on their website as a tool for developing differentiation opportunities for more-able pupils. It is popularly used at KS 3 and has been extensively documented in supporting younger learners. The journal *Gifted Education International* has published a double issue documenting the various recent TASC applications (Vol. 24 Nos 2 and 3. (2008) AB Academic Publishers.) Belle Wallace has also used the TASC Framework to support her own masters and PhD students. In the light of the extensive applications of the TASC Framework at all phases of education, TASC would seem to be the ideal framework to support the development of independent learning for AS and A2 students. Let us consider the segments of the Wheel again and how they can be issued in supporting an AS or A2 student. For greater clarification refer to Figure 2.1 (with kind permission).

1. *Gather/Organize* (What do I already know?): This stage encourages students to value the knowledge they already have and to set a research framework based upon what questions they wish to ask and to answer.
2. *Identify* (What is my task?): Defining the task clearly helps students to focus on the key questions and to engage with the conceptual and knowledge foci of the task.
3. *Generate* (How many ideas can I think if?): This stage encourages the students to be creative in their thinking. They are generating the ideas, not the teacher, thus supporting the independent nature of their own learning. Students are setting their own

Figure 2.1 TASC wheel

learning goals and embarking upon their self-defined learning journey.

4. *Decide* (Which is the best way?): Decision-making can be individually completed or agreed in consultation with peers or a teacher. The connection students develop with the decision-making process ensures that they have ownership over the process and final product of the task. In other words the task has not been imposed on the students and is not something being 'done to them'. At every level the work belongs to the student.

5. *Implement* (Let's do it!): This is often the hardest aspect of the work – to actually get on and do it. How to approach this may require its own support frameworks to begin with, and this may be the steepest learning curve for many students, but with the use of scaffolds, as suggested earlier, the implementing stage will become more autonomous over time.

6. *Evaluate* (How well have I done?): Chapter Three explores evaluation scaffolding, and argues that it is desirable to encourage

AS and A2 students to become reflective learners, and this evaluative stage of the TASC Framework encourages students to evaluate not only the outcomes of their work but the process by which they arrived there. This self- and peer-assessment of learning is a key stepping stone for reaching the goal of independent learning.

7. *Communicate* (How can I share?): As discussed in Chapter One, sharing their findings can be challenging for many students. This segment of the TASC Wheel is more than just a means of telling someone what they have learned; it also encourages students to clarify their learning and to identify any gaps and to return to other parts of the TASC Wheel for possible 're-thinking'. This encourages the student to further develop their critical learning and self-awareness.

8. *Learn from experience* (What have I learned?): This stage is the reflective and consolidation section of the whole TASC process. Next steps can be set for future independent learning tasks based on the finding of this part of the learning process.

A Classics AS topic of the 'Fall of the Roman Empire 81–31BC' could be independently studied using the TASC framework with the task of assessing the extent of political conflict in this period. Students may have already investigated Cicero's speeches and the teacher wishes students to extend this to wider political conflict in the period and the relationship between Cicero and Caesar. A student schedule using the TACS framework may appear as under.

1. *Gather/Organize*: Share prior learning, identify gaps in knowledge.
2. *Identify*: Consider the task and what will be required of a study relating to political conflict; contextual understanding is necessary.
3. *Generate*: Students will ask questions of the task and topic and determine a final outcome.
4. *Decide*: A route through the work will be agreed and work plan devised with agreed tasks, resources and deadlines.
5. *Implement*: Students begin the work, prepared to ask for help if required.
6. *Evaluate*: Regular progress checks and alteration of the work plan will be required.
7. *Communicate*: Agree an audience to share findings with.

8. *Learn from Experience*: Reflect on process and results of learning in order to improve in both areas next time.

An alternative framework for independent learning is discussed in the Oxford Brooks PIPAR Case Studies and is referred to as the TULIP model definition. This model appears to offer a greater level of construction for student planning and thinking with a hierarchical ladder of 'stages to thinking'. This model has a greater clarity for some learners and allows them to plan their learning journey in a more linear fashion. Learners begin by making a 'decision' about the topic of study and its objectives and then determining what they are going to do and how they are going to do it. A cyclical route of 'finding' and 'organizing' follows as learners build the knowledge base and organize their research to support the decisions made at the outset of the process. Once findings are organized, learners can 'develop' their ideas to exemplify their initial decision and task foci. After development is complete, learners are in a position to present their results and finally evaluate their end product and learning journey. For many this is a less complex framework for independent learning and can serve as an initial scaffold for independent learning especially at AS level. Consider the 'stages in thinking' again and how they can be used in supporting AS or A2 students.

1. *Deciding*: The students are encouraged to examine the facets of the task from the very outset and determine what is required of them in regard to content, skills and conceptual understanding.
2. *Finding*: This research aspect of the task will encourage students to employ independent reading and research skills using providing and independently determined material.
3. *Organizing*: This can be a challenging aspect of individual learning especially when decision-making is required over what information to keep and how to utilize findings. The limitations of acquired knowledge and understanding will help students to independently determine where further learning is required.
4. *Developing*: This encourages the students to process the organized knowledge and deal with conceptual and skills based learning. Analysis will take place in this stage of thinking.
5. *Presenting*: Students will need to consider their intended audience and how to present their information in an informed and engaging manner.

6. *Evaluating*: This will help the students to reflect on the methodology of their work and the learning journey they have embarked upon. Next steps for independent learning can be set at this stage as well as in relation to the task and topic being studied.

Both models offer more than a scaffold; they offer an approach to independent learning that facilitates the steps students need to follow in order to become independent learners, as well as encouraging opportunities for reflection on their learning and how they learned. Experienced independent learners will be able to identify their learning needs, plan how the learning will take place and evaluate their learning against agreed success criteria. AS and A2 students will need support, guidance and built-in opportunities for evaluation of their strengths and target areas in mastering such techniques. Models such as TULIP and TASC can make that process a more manageable and achievable one. Through regular evaluation and comparison of how each framework is working, students are encouraged to evaluate their method of working as well as the final product. It is a good idea to ask students if they have used this approach to learning in other lessons and to discuss their strengths and weaknesses. Discussing how students can improve their independent learning can lead to them making a personal progression chart to ensure they are becoming more advanced in their approach to working independently.

Summary

Independent learning will not occur naturally; it will require planning and facilitating. This can be structured in a variety of ways and the two models provided offer a suggested route for students. Many students will be familiar with working independently and it is important to ascertain the current position of each student before embarking upon independent learning. The earlier occasions of independent learning may not prove as successful as you may hope and it is important to not give up at this point but to evaluate why the work did not succeed and move forward from this point. If 'failure' is brushed aside and the process never revisited the students' development as independent learners will be damaged in the long term.

12. Using Information and Communication Technology (ICT) to support independent learning

This section will highlight uses of ICT to promote independent learning for AS and A2 students. This is not intended as a guide to ICT but suggests areas of ICT which can help to students to act and work more independently. Turn to the references section for further reading in ICT-specific teaching and learning books to support this area of expertise and promote innovative ideas in ICT across all subjects.

Independent learning can often be misconstrued by students and teachers as a research based activity with a 'go away and find out' approach given to children from as early as KS2. This methodology is often used with no real guidance or direction of how to do this. Children as young as six will usually wish to turn to the internet as their first point of reference for information. They enter key words in search engines and use the first website presented to them. It is easy to assume that 'A' Level students have the necessary skills to use a more sophisticated and systematic method of research on the internet, with more precise key words as well as an ability to discriminate between the uses of websites based on the intended audience of the website. This belief is reinforced by the 2004 National Curriculum which asserts that from 11 years of age pupils have a statutory requirement to study research skills in their ICT lessons. The National Curriculum KS3 (Revised 2004) Programme of Study for Information and communication technology 1b states 'Pupils should be taught how to obtain information well matched to purpose by selecting appropriate sources, using and refining search methods and questioning the plausibility and value of the information found.' The National Curriculum 2007 programme of study for Information and Communication Technology has developed this further and has stipulated that pupils need to understand 'capability' as a concept in ICT, with the requirement of 1.1a 'Using a range of ICT tools in a purposeful way to tackle questions, solve problems and create ideas of solution and value.' Further to this, the same document identifies 'critical evaluation' as a key concept and requires students have an understanding in 'Recognising that information must not be taken at face value, but must be analysed and evaluated to take account of its purpose, author, currency and context.' The key processes of finding information, developing ideas, communicating information and evaluating are also being taught to 11-year olds across England and Wales from

September 2008. This is a giant leap forward for all students in terms of their ICT capabilities as independent learners. However as with all learning skills, teachers must not take for granted that students are in possession of such capability and even at AS level they may make inefficient use of the internet as an independent research tool. If students are being asked to research independently ensure whether the correct tools are in place for them to do this and as with all independent learning structures discussed in this chapter, build a scaffold into lessons which can be steadily dismantled throughout the year.

It must be clearly stated however that independent learning using ICT reaches far beyond a research activity on the internet. With many colleges and Sixth Forms adopting a virtual learning environment (VLE) the possibilities for learning away from the direction of the teacher have become much more extensive. Local authorities are signing up to the principles and practicalities of a VLE with a view to creating localized e-learning communities and encouraging students to work beyond the classroom. Consult with your IT technician as to where your institution is currently at, in terms of adopting a VLE and access any local training to utilize it to the maximum potential.

The purpose of a VLE is to enable remote and interactive teaching and learning. A class page can be created to encourage students to engage in conversation regarding a particular topic or to share their research findings or test a given hypothesis. All these activities require the student to be proactive in their learning and to take the initiative in posting ideas or resources and responding to the suggestions and comments of others in a very exposed environment. A more independent-minded student may seize the moment and launch their own investigation through the VLE and via the use of blogs and forums the teacher can find themselves on the outside of a student-led discussion.

Publishers are well aware of the students' capacity to work independently on their PC and are moving towards CD-ROM support as an integral part of a text book in many subject areas. Many of these CD-ROMs encourage students to explore themes and questions raised in the text books without the prior authorization of their teacher. Tasks and games aim to make learning 'fun' for the student but more fundamentally encourage them to experiment with their learning away from the confines of the classroom and whilst not under the teacher lens. Mistakes can be made without repercussion and topics explored and revisited at leisure. Similar resources such as network enabled CD-ROMs and online journals are worth investigation and will encourage students to take ownership of their learning and develop the hungry and enquiring mind many teachers aim for in their students.

Summary

Virtual learning environments (VLEs) are an ideal vehicle to encourage group and independent learning and move responsibility for learning away from the teacher towards the student. Setting up a virtual classroom may require initial support for the e-learning coordinator and IT technician but once established and mastered uploading and monitoring need not be onerous. Ask a different student to take responsibility for aspects of the VLE each month and make use of it within lessons and for homework to increase its value and purpose.

Chapter summary

Students are often cosseted in the classroom by well-meaning and experienced teachers who only want the best for their students. By taking sole responsibility for their learning teachers disengage students from the more stimulating cognitive and meta-cognitive aspects of the subject and learning. At 16 students are in a position to take responsibility for their own learning with their teacher to guide and support them. Independence can be achieved through a range of strategies. It will require thought and planning and may take a year to achieve but the interaction that will result between teacher and student will create a truly captivated class.

3 | Encouraging reflective learners

Formative assessment is defined as . . . frequent, interactive assessments of student progress and understanding to identify learning needs and adjust teaching appropriately.

OECD Study, 2005

Assessment is a fundamental aspect of post-16 education. Primarily assessment takes the form of summative assessment through a rigid external examination process. Examination processes are rigorously moderated to ensure consistency across the country in all subjects. Results are published and Sixth Form centres and colleges are compared against each other via achievement and attainment tables based on statistical pass rates and student averages. Examination results are used as a performance indicator for teachers' performance management profiles and parents look to examination results as an indicator of the quality of education their children are likely to receive in an education establishment.

The move towards an AS and A2 system of examinations in 2000 increased the frequency of examinations sat by post-16 students although the recent shift towards fewer examination papers at level 3 qualifications including AS and A2 has alleviated the examination burden to some extent. Due to this emphasis on examination results Sixth form leaders and teachers are explicitly aware of the importance of achieving good grades for their students and most teachers will do everything they can to ensure examination success.

Unfortunately the drive to achieve examination success has arguably had a detrimental affect on the teaching and learning which takes place in many AS and A2 classrooms. The emphasis on examination techniques and preparation has led to what is commonly known as 'spoon-feeding' students in order that they can pass the exam. The important consequences of AS and A2 summative assessment has been shown by Brooks to 'narrow the curriculum gap and encourage rote learning; widen the gap between high and low achievers;

promote high anxiety levels and erode self-esteem.' Teachers view it as their responsibility to provide students with knowledge, examination tips and structures that result in formulaic approaches to examination questions. This can result in a reduced emphasis on subject discipline as well as a dampened passion for learning. Many teachers feel trapped by the external pressures placed upon them and wish to free up their curriculum to explore their subject in greater depth than a syllabus allows.

In 1998 Paul Black and Dylan Wiliam published Inside the Black Box a treatise that set out to challenge the use of assessment in classrooms nationwide. They purported the idea that greater use of formative assessment in classrooms would improve teaching and learning and raise standards. Their work became a turning point in education and since 1998 research, piloting and implementation of formative assessment has taken place through the KMOFAP project, the National Strategy and most recently through the personalization agenda. Assessment for Learning as it has become commonly known is a process undertaken in partnership with teachers and students to enable students to understand the learning process they are involved in and how to get better within that process. This can also be defined as 'reflective learning'; developing the skills within students to enable them to question and determine their own ability, progress and steps to improvement.

This chapter will seek to explore what assessment for learning means within a post-16 environment, when the assessment stakes are regarded as 'high' and how teachers can employ and make use of formative assessment techniques in order to captivate their class and place the ownership of learning firmly in the hands of the students.

13. Understanding of performance and how to improve

Assessment in education must, first and foremost, serve the purpose of supporting learning.

Paul Black and Dylan Wiliam 2006

In 2003 the Assessment Reform Group 2003 published their research based Principles of Assessment for Learning. They are summarized below Assessment for learning is most effective when it:

◆ Part of effective planning;
◆ Focuses on how students learn;
◆ Central to classroom practice;

◆ A key professional skill;
◆ Sensitive and constructive;
◆ Fosters motivation;
◆ Promotes understanding of goals and criteria;
◆ Helps learners know how to improve;
◆ Develops the capacity for self-assessment;
◆ Recognizes all educational achievement.

In 2006 the KS3 National Strategy redefined Assessment for Learning key characteristics as:

◆ using effective questioning techniques;
◆ using marking and feedback strategies;
◆ sharing learning goals;
◆ peer and self-assessment.

This is an all encompassing agenda. Schools and colleges could not ignore the importance of assessment for learning in moving teaching and learning forward, in England and Wales. More recent DCSF initiatives of personalized learning have further embraced the importance of assessment for learning in establishing appropriate individual pathways for learning. At its conception personalization was sometimes confused with individualization, where students work individually or are left to their own devices. This is a misunderstanding of personalization which Christine Gilbert in the DCSF 2020 Vision paper describes as a 'highly structured and responsive approach'. Personalization makes use of the Every Child Matters agenda to provide a pathway through school that is pertinent and responsive to the social, emotional and learning needs of every individual student. Assessment for learning is the most critical tool in developing and personalizing an individual student's route through school, as it takes account of the specific learning needs of each student. Similarly, at the heart of gifted and talented education, as explored in Chapter Four, is the use of assessment for learning to provide insight into the potential and actual needs of more-able students. It is through assessment for learning that a teacher and student come to a purposeful understanding of the individual's learning needs.

Assessment for learning in schools is not only about ensuring these aspects of the assessment for learning agenda are taking place within lessons; it is asking teachers to make use of these foci to learn more about their students within a class and encourage these same students to learn more about themselves. Formative assessment is not to be a bolted on activity that takes place at regular intervals; instead formative assessment is to be an intrinsic aspect of every lesson that takes place in every classroom. Across a unit of study students are to be given clear objectives so that they can understand and move forward from summative data, make use of criteria and feedback and engage in peer and self-assessment.

Many teachers have embraced some or all of these assessment for learning principles yet 'A' Level classrooms due to their 'high stakes' learning have in many instances lagged behind their primary and secondary counterparts . This is due in part to the reluctance of many teachers to experiment with these initiatives for fear of not meeting syllabus requirements and leaving students ill-prepared for the exam. Yet it is in 'high stakes' learning more than any other that all assessment for learning techniques can actively involve students in their own learning and motivate their desire to learn as well as prepare them for the examination. The means to achieving reflective learners is through a shift in educators' mindsets from regarding the teacher solely as a provider of knowledge and moving towards the acknowledgement of the teacher as also being a facilitator of student learning. This philosophical shift will take commitment and time and with a DCSF shift towards greater school partnerships and a potential reduction in the importance of attainment and achievement tables as a result of the 14–19 agenda, it is entirely achievable.

The rest of this chapter will set out how assessment for learning techniques can be effectively employed in 'A' Level classrooms to the benefit of all involved.

Summary

Assessment for learning can allow teachers to know and guide all their students as individual learners. It has many facets and is a complex process that is more than grades and levels. Assessment for learning is most effective when its many aspects become integral to everyday teaching and learning and make up a framework of student classroom provision. This is not an overnight shift and requires patience, commitment and professional learning on the part of the teacher. Figure 3.1 demonstrates how the different aspects of assessment for learning link together.

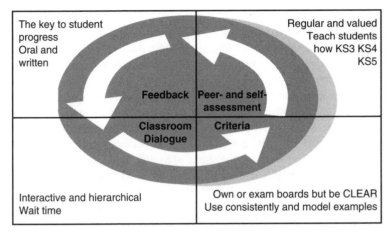

Figure 3.1 The different aspects of assessment for learning link together

14. Questioning

Questioning . . . led to richer discourse, in which the teachers evoked a wealth of information from which to judge the current level of understanding of their students. More importantly, they had evidence on which to plan the next steps in learning so the challenge and pace of lessons could be directed by formative assessment evidence rather than simply following a prescribed agenda.

Black, Harrison, Lee, Marshall and Wiliam (2003)

This quote identifies the central importance of questioning in assessing and planning for student learning. In an 'A' Level classroom how often can the 'prescribed agenda' determine lesson planning and student learning rather than the needs of the individual student. Whilst it is acknowledged throughout this book that teachers of AS and A2 students have a duty to deliver a specification and syllabus they also have a responsibility to help their students 'get better' at their subject. Questioning serves dual purpose in helping a teacher meet course requirements and in developing subject mastery and progress.

Strategies to support student dialogue have been addressed in Chapter One. Questioning is a means of developing and extending student dialogue and is an essential tool for both teaching and learning. Questions can be used orally and in written form but for the purposes of this section and their place in developing reflective learning the emphasis will be on oral questioning. Teachers fall into three categories when reflecting upon their skills of questioning. The first and rarest group are able to practice questioning in an instinctive and intuitive manner and can lead and direct questioning with little advance consideration. The second and most dominant group believe they can use questioning instinctively and intuitively and therefore do not plan for it. The final group recognize that questioning is a significant feature of a lesson and is of great benefit to student learning and accordingly requires advance planning and consideration of hierarchy and method. It is worth spending a moment to reflect which category your 'A' Level teaching falls into.

Effective questioning is a skill that cannot be regarded highly enough and when it is executed well students are able to feel secure in their subject knowledge, tackle problems with clear expectations and at a deeper level and develop independence: all qualities a teacher would look for in effective assessment for learning. Questioning is a skill that can be learned and successfully executed through the use of simple techniques and through a deeper understanding of lesson objectives and subject progression.

In an 'A' Level classroom questioning is arguably of even greater importance in terms of developing subject knowledge, moving learning forward and building self-esteem. 'A' Level classes can be smaller than 11–16 classes and provide a more intimate environment to develop dialogue at a more personalized level. When planned for within the structure of a lesson and allocated the appropriate amount of lesson times, all students within the lesson can be involved in moving their learning forward. Questioning will be considered in two ways within this section:

1. practical methodology of executing questions;
2. planning a hierarchy of questions to extend student thinking.

Practical methodology of executing questions

Wait Time. There is a wealth of evidence on how teachers use questioning within the classroom. Some of the most well known is based around the research of Rowe in 1974. Her study into the elementary science classes in the USA investigated classroom discourse and found that the mean time between teachers asking a question and waiting for an answer was 0.9 seconds. More recently Stahl relabelled 'wait time' to 'think time' to reinforce the purpose of silence was for students to be able to complete on task thinking. Research as recent as 2007 reinforces that the average wait time for a teacher in a classroom between asking a question and moving on is 1–3 seconds. Consider this within an AS or A2 teaching environment. A student is asked a question and the expectation is for the student to answer quickly. The messages that this sends out about learning contradicts expectations of other learning strategies. The principle goal of questioning appears to be speed; silence is not acceptable, thinking is not valued and formulating a coherent response is not given appreciation. Very few teachers would consider these desirable goals yet they are enforced across many post-16 classrooms through rapid fire questioning techniques with little 'wait time' by the teacher for a response. Rowe went on to look at the effect of increasing 'wait time' and found the following changes in pupil learning took place:

◆ answers were longer;
◆ failure to respond decreased;
◆ responses were more confident;
◆ students challenged;
◆ alternative explanations were offered.

These are attractive learning goals and achievable by increasing the 'wait time' between posing a question and accepting an answer. The length of 'wait time' should vary according to the level of difficulty the question poses. A comprehension question may require 1–2 seconds and an evaluative question could require up to 30 seconds (question hierarchies are discussed later). In a post-16 environment anxieties about disruption and student's switching off due to a prolonged 'wait time' should not be of concern, it will however take students a little while to adapt to this approach and it is worth explaining why you are waiting in order that the students use the time purposefully. 'Wait time' also means that it is realistic for the teacher to expect a response from all students and therefore the 'no-hands' rule can be employed.

No-hands. This is a fixed rule within my own 'A' Level teaching and students are expected to abide by it from lesson one. At its simplest level 'no-hands' means exactly that – students are not allowed to raise their hand in answer to a question; they are expected to be prepared to offer an answer and if they cannot they must say they do not know. The learning processes which take place within this simple rule are however far more complex.

- ◆ No-hands has to become a classroom culture (it must be used all the time).
- ◆ It cannot work without 'wait time'.
- ◆ Question repetition may be required and does not indicate a student was not listening simply that they needed question clarification.
- ◆ It requires students to feel comfortable in being able to admit they do not have an answer.
- ◆ Interaction between teacher-student and student-student needs to be secure and respectful.
- ◆ There is nowhere to hide and it becomes mandatory for students to be actively involved in the questioning process.
- ◆ It alerts the teacher to the relative progress and understanding of each student.
- ◆ It alerts the student to their learning gaps and need for intervention.
- ◆ A range of other talking strategies (e.g. think, pair, share) need to be used to help support student responses (see Chapter One).

Target or Broadcast. This strategy works well alongside no-hands and is an invaluable assessment for learning tool in terms of the teacher gauging different levels of students' understanding. The teacher either targets the question to a specified individual or group of individuals or the question is broadcast for all students to answer. Targeted questioning is effectively used at 'A' Level when it is aimed to consolidate learning and assess who has understood which aspects of the lesson objectives. It requires sensitivity and should not be used to catch students out or humiliate them but it can help the teacher to determine next steps in learning on an individual basis. The damage to self-esteem could simply be too great to overcome. Broadcast questions can be used to introduce topics or concepts and move learning forward, they help generate discussion and responses can be praised, rephrased, corrected or extended by the student or teacher.

- ◆ *Praise* remains an essential form of confidence building within an 'A' Level classroom but students will not be able to make progress without also being informed of when have not grasped the full meaning of the area of study or have completely misunderstood.

◆ *Rephrase* does not mean repeating a student's comment using your own words; students can rephrase each other's comments to consolidate learning. A different use of language and vocabulary can improve an answer further and generate further reflection on the importance of appropriate and subject-specific vocabulary.

◆ *Correct* inaccurate comments and responses; positive reinforcement of misunderstandings are not helpful and can cause future cognitive conflict.

◆ *Extend* the most helpful type of classroom discourse; the only response allowed is one which extends another contribution. Extension can mean contradiction and alternative answers.

Ping Pong Versus Basketball. Consider the following classroom scenario; the teacher is at the front of the classroom asking questions of the class, he throws them back and forth to the students using a range of targeted and broadcast questions. Each answer is directed back to the teacher and commented upon before the teacher bats another question to the class. The physical appearance of the questioning resembles a game of ping pong with the teacher holding one bat and the rest of the class the other. The teacher is doing everything previously mentioned and hierarchical questions have been planned yet the class is becoming bored and the teacher is left exhausted. In the classroom next door a second teacher has also planned his/her questioning and is using a no-hands approach to engage as many students as possible. This time the teacher does not respond to students' comments; the discourse is open for comment from all students as praise, rephrasing, correction and extension are passed back and forth between the teacher and the students. The teacher intervenes at well-judged moments based on their expertise and professional judgement. The physical appearance of the questioning resembles a game of basketball with the teacher passing and catching the ball as and when his team members pass to him or he steals the ball from another player. The teacher is part of a whole class activity in which all students are engaged and responsive. The teacher is censoring less and probing more thus encouraging development of student understanding. It is challenging to adopt a basketball approach to questioning when teachers have traditionally played ping pong with their class. This can be achieved by emphasizing the classroom culture with the students, where the class is immersed in the questioning culture for all the facets to work in unison.

Planning a hierarchy of questions to extend student thinking

Why does a teacher use questions in the classroom? Does the teacher always plan to use questions in the classroom and if so, are those questions prepared in advance? Teachers ask questions for many reasons, ranging from less demanding comprehension and recall questions to synthesis and evaluation questions making greater cognitive demands of the student. The hierarchy of questioning is often based on a theoretical base such as Bloom's taxonomy (discussed in Chapter Four). Bloom wanted to show that thinking worked on different levels and that by adapting the style and nature of questions asked, teachers can induce higher levels of thinking. A teacher can mistakenly believe they need to work though the hierarchy in a linear fashion every lesson or sequence of lessons but it would be wasteful of learning time to use a spectrum of hierarchical questioning as wide ranging as Bloom suggests every lesson. It could take a student many years to progress into the higher-order domain and the cognitive range of the questions used should aim to reflect the intended learning outcomes. Husband's (1996) makes this point in his research by making the point that the emphasis of questioning should not be on the hierarchy of difficulty but on using different types of questions to support different ways of thinking. The emphasis in an 'A' Level classroom should be on the lesson intentions and how the questioning used can enable students to meet those objectives. If the lesson emphasis is on acquiring knowledge there will be greater attention to comprehension style question. If the lesson is focusing on reflection different question stems will be employed to elicit the required outcome from the students. Similarly if the lesson focus is linked to making judgements a different set of question types will be employed. Questions need to be prepared in advance of a lesson in order to ensure that lesson objectives can be met. The lesson objectives therefore need to go beyond a content based delivery and focus on the skills and concepts that students are aiming to develop. When objectives are clearly defined effective use of questioning can be made to secure student understanding in this area. Planning is essential, as is the strategic use of questioning with students and finally the following consolidation of learning which follows in subsequent lessons. A range of question stems to support different phases of learning are suggested below and can be applied to most subject areas.

Knowledge and Comprehension. Who...? Which...? When...? What...?

Who put forward a counter-argument in passage C? (Critical thinking)
Which artists does your work make connections with? (Art and Design)
When did you notice a reaction between the chemicals in your experiment? (Chemistry)
What were the conclusions to each investigation? (Geography)

Application and Analysis. Why...? How else...? What effect...?

Why did you choose that material for your final product design? (Design and technology)
How else might the corporate objectives of M&S plc change over time? (Business Studies)
What effect does the author use lexis and register to construct the narrators voice? (English Language and Literature)

Synthesis and Evaluation. How far...? What if...? How similar...?

How far are traditional arguments in the existence of God valid in the 21st century? (Religious Studies)
What would happen if all the world's computers were attacked by a super-virus? (Information technology)
How similar are the reactions to the Iraq and Vietnam wars? (International Relations)

A final note on questioning relates to the use of vocabulary and clarity of the question. Open and closed questions are well documented but consider the following.

♦ Are the questions you are asking, steering students into a particular path of answering or are the questions allowing for the reflection you are aiming for?
♦ Is the question using subject-specific vocabulary and language to generate the level of thinking you are aiming for?
♦ Is the question you are asking encouraging students to think of an answer themselves as opposed to seeking out what they think will be the 'right' answer?

Questions can often be written with a pre-determined answer in mind especially at 'A' Level when mark schemes often define a 'correct' answer. Ensure there is scope for individuality in the questions you ask. Phrasing questions can be time consuming and difficult but when the answer to the question reflects a student's own thinking then the question was a good one.

Summary

Questioning is a vital skill within an AS and A2 classroom and allows students to explore and articulate their own understanding as well as challenge others' thinking. Questioning can introduce, develop and consolidate areas of study as well as raise and crush students' self esteem. There are few other classroom practices that are so universal in their characteristics. Questions are most effective when planned in advance and meet the learning objectives of the lesson. In an 'A' Level environment this will require thought and deeper understanding of the foci of your intended outcome. Well-structured questions in a supportive environment can move student learning forward at an accelerated pace and create a culture for learning in which all are involved.

15. Feedback – Feeding back and feeding forward

Feedback to any pupil should be about the particular qualities of his or her work, with advice on what he or she can do to improve, and should avoid comparisons with other pupils. Feedback has shown to improve learning where it gives each pupil specific guidance on strengths and weaknesses, preferably without any overall marks.

Inside the Black Box, *Black and Wiliam (1998)*

The most powerful single moderator that enhances achievement is feedback.

Hattie (1992)

Feedback is a highly contentious issue. Many teachers and school leaders confuse feedback with marking and though the two are inter-related they can serve quite different purposes. The focus of this chapter is reflective learners and it is feedback (in which marking plays a role), more than any aspect of assessment for learning, that can enable a student to be reflective and understand their next steps for learning.

To clarify these positions consider my own definition of both terms.

Marking students' work involves passing a judgement on their work and measuring against an internally or externally imposed benchmarking system. Marking allows students to gain a sense of performance against a set criteria and offers a more summative approach to assessing a student's progress. If a student is aware of their target grade they can determine whether they are on target to meet it and plan their future learning upon their current and pre-dicted performance. It is an important tool for the student and teacher and is of greatest benefit when used sparingly and purpose-fully, termly assessments and mock examinations, for example.

Feedback is the information communicated to a student in regard to their understanding of shared learning objectives of a given task against an agreed set of criteria. This information will include guid-ance on how to improve. Feedback is the information that is relayed to the student about their progress and can be based upon a variety of forms of evidence including: marked work, un-graded teacher checked worked, oral contribution, practical displays, draft work and re-drafted work. This information can be relayed to the student in a written comment or in a face to face discussion. It is widely agreed to be the single most determining factor in enabling student to make progress and is recognized as such through the personalization agenda.

Both are essential yet are regarded very differently. Marking can be viewed very negatively by teachers and students. Teachers find it time consuming in terms of the return gains from students. Students feel an over-emphasis can be placed on grades and marks, reinforcing failure with little regard to the needs of the individual student. (Butler 1988, Black and Wiliam 1998, LEARN project 2000).

In schools and colleges, school leaders can become obsessed by the need for teacher marking to support tracking systems and monitor student progress, pressure is placed on middle leaders to ensure their departments are marking and teachers are monitored and become stressed by the whole experience. Yet few school leaders and teachers would dispute the value of feedback.

So how can marking become more manageable and be used more supportively in feeding back information to students that they can feed forward in their learning? This section will attempt to explore a range of strategies that will make this achievable.

Shirley Clarke recommends selective marking and a range of marking strategies to ensure feedback be given promptly and with clear criteria-driven focus. Her techniques were not initially devised for use at post-16 but having employed Clarke's techniques post -16 for several years they have made my marking manageable and my feedback purposeful. Below are a few of her suggestions.

◆ *Grading*: Yes but be selective and use when necessary for example, in summative assessments. For quality assurance ensure departmental consistency and share grade criteria with the students.
◆ *Acknowledgement marking*: At times a straightforward recognition of work being completed in the form of a simple tick, stamp or signature is all that is required. This is most likely to be student notes or work that has been peer or self-marked. At 'A' Level a large bulk of information based work can be acknowledged this way.
◆ *Sampling*: The idea of sampling is to improve manageability of marking work load. It can take the form of marking a few

students' work in depth and applying general trends from the sample to assist all students in a peer marking exercise or using a sample as the basis for a one-to-one feedback tutorial. OfSTED recognizes this as a successful method of managing marking. 'The problem of manageability is being tackled successfully in some schools through systems for staggering marking or sampling' (OfSTED 2003). In an 'A' Level class this could be based around target grades and focusing on the A/B grades one week, C grades the next and so on. Alternatively a spread of work may be marked and then marking modelled for peer assessment.

◆ *Marking together*: This can be used effectively to gauge understanding when there are clear right and wrong answers such as in Maths or Modern Foreign Languages. The teacher can feed forward the results to plan next steps.

◆ *Comment only*: This technique avoids any grading or scoring of work and concentrates on the success of the work and the areas for improvement in both individual pieces and for meeting the learning objectives over a longer period of time. The comments are based on specific task criteria and not on all aspects of the work in order to ensure purposeful and manageable marking for the teacher and to be helpful to the student receiving the comments. Comment only marking can be especially effective when students embark upon a new AS or A2 course when initially grades would be meaningless and demoralizing. It also enables students to gain a more thorough understanding of the particular skill or concept they are trying to improve in. The nature and phrasing of the targets set are discussed in Section 16. Comments need to be delivered promptly and in a language students can understand and act upon. Comments also need to be specifically related to the task criteria and avoid generalizations. Opportunities to address the targets set need to be built into the lesson in which the work is returned and again in future lessons through revisiting the same learning objective.

Shirley Clarke's work in this field (2005) suggests a 3:1 approach of success: improvement comments. Most 'A' Level students can arguably cope with a more even ratio. For example, two or three areas of the work that have met the pre-determined and shared criteria are indicated through highlighting or underling with a brief comment as to how these meet the criteria in order that the student can use these areas of their work for future modelling. Two or a maximum of three areas of the work requiring improvement are then indicated with a stamp or star and a noted with a target for improvement. (See Section 16 for examples of comments.) Improved work should be acknowledged and praised at the earliest opportunity.

Feedback is most effective when it is delivered promptly and reflection time is planned into the lesson to allow students time to respond to the comment and if possible act upon it immediately. By delaying feedback students forget the original purpose of the work and the challenges they faced when completing it. The pace of learning depreciates if a student is moving onto another task before receiving feedback on the former piece of work. Consider a diligent Year 12 student called Kerry who has spent many hours preparing her chemistry experiment analysis; she is proud of her work and hopes the teacher is pleased with her efforts; Kerry struggled to explain the inconsistencies in her experiment; she hands it in on time and awaits her teacher's feedback. Three lessons pass and no comment is made to the Kerry by the teacher, Kerry is too polite to ask as she appreciates that the teacher is busy. In the next lesson the class conducts a similar experiment to the previous one and in the write up that follows Kerry yet again finds it difficult to explain an inconsistency in her data and begins to worry that she is not very good at this aspect of chemistry. This is not an unusual story and on the surface not a very interesting one but on reflection Kerry is in danger of losing motivation as her self-esteem is being damaged by a lack of communication from her teacher. Kerry was pleased with her work yet it was unacknowledged and not praised, she required help but did not feel secure enough to ask and by not receiving prompt feedback Kerry was unable to improve her work when a similar task was undertaken. By reading Kerry's work her teacher would have identified the area Kerry was struggling with and supported her with this aspect of the second piece of work. Teacher and Kerry would have worked together on improving her explanation and Kerry's self-esteem would be intact. Prompt feedback matters.

The impact of prompt, criteria based feedback on selected pieces of work will have greater long-term impact on a student's learning and their results and is of greater benefit than an inadequate attempt to mark everything in detail at irregular intervals. Time and opportunities for feedback need to be planned into a teacher and students lesson schedule in order to maximize its impact. Post-16 teachers sometimes remark that they cannot afford to spare lesson time for students to respond to feedback as there is too much content to get through. If some of the strategies from Chapter One are employed and content is not longer the only focus of lesson planning and objectives then there will be time. The students will make progress as a consequence of being allocated time to reflect on how they need to improve.

Consider which of the following will make a greater impact on student learning and achievement: thirty minutes spent reflecting upon and addressing clearly defined targets for improvement or thirty minutes cramming a lesson with content?

A Summary of the key principles

Comment only marking

◆ Comments are phrased positively.
◆ Comments are subject specific, identify success and ways to improve learning.
◆ Individual targets are set.
◆ Targets are monitored by student and teacher.
◆ Reflection time is included in feedback lessons.

Written feedback

◆ Focuses on the learning objectives selectively.
◆ Confirms that students are on the right track.
◆ Stimulates the correction of errors or improvement of a piece of work.
◆ Scaffolds or supporting students' next steps.
◆ Provides opportunities for students to think things through for themselves.
◆ Comments on progress over a number of attempts.
◆ Avoids comparisons with other students.
◆ Provides students with the opportunities to respond.

The suggestions and strategies offered so far are based on written feedback but ideally feedback will be a combination of oral and written information and guidance to help a teacher and student plan the next steps in a student's learning. Oral feedback has one advantage above written feedback, primarily the immediacy of the comment. In oral feedback a student is told immediately how they need to improve. In a face to face environment body language and choice of words and phrases will be crucial to how the student interprets your comment. Teachers should always praise a student as well as offer specific details of ways to move forward. Questioning can incorporate feedback and the structure of questioning (as discussed in Section 15) can feedforward the feedback from students' work or a previous lesson. Opportunities to speak one to one to 'A' Level students can be difficult; to overcome this problem a sampling approach can be successful. Allocate part of the lesson, where students are working independently to discuss feedback and next steps' learning with a small group of students with similar areas for improvement. Peer discussion can also be used for feedback purposes and is discussed in Section 17.

Summary

To summarize the conventions of oral feedback should follow those of written and at the heart of the feedback should be the individual student and what they need to do to become a better student of your subject. Ideally a college or school will have a feedback policy and the importance of feedback for student progress will be acknowledged through whole college system. An example of a whole school feedback policy is shown in Table 3.1. How does this compare to your college or department policy? Are there ideas within this that can be employed to make your marking manageable and your feedback worthy of feeding forward into students' learning?

Table 3.1 An example of a whole school feedback policy

Aims of feedback for students	Aims of feedback for teachers	Key principles of effective feedback
◆ To evaluate their progress	◆ To monitor progress	◆ Directly links to the shared outcomes
◆ To work towards and meet targets	◆ To set work related and personal targets	◆ Is prompt
◆ To understand marking criteria	◆ To measure learning and understanding	◆ Is phrased positively
◆ To maximize their own potential	◆ To maximize student potential	◆ Shows next steps
◆ To be rewarded for their success	◆ To improve literacy	◆ Is built in to reflection time
◆ To move students forward	◆ To mark effectively and efficiently	

Criteria	Comments	Frequency
1. Criteria for marking are identified in planning and clearly communicated to the students	1. Comments are phrased positively	1. Student books/folders are teacher checked at least every six lessons
2. Policy is shared with students in exercise books	2. Comments are subject specific, identify success and ways to improve learning	2. A minimum of three formal assessment per year group per term
3. Subject progression, level and grading criteria are shared with students	3. Individual targets are set	3. Homework is acknowledged immediately
4. Peer- and self-assessment opportunities are included in each taught module	4. Targets are monitored by student and teacher	4. Policy is consistently used across departments and this is supported by half-termly monitoring procedures
5. Reward policy is in line with that agreed at the text box 'A Summary of the Key Principles	5. Reflection time is included in feedback lessons	5. Subject leaders will discuss departmental feedback with their line managers every half term

16. Target setting

Section 15 discusses the benefits of comment only marking and the impact effective feedback can have on AS and A2 students' learning. Such strategies will only be successful however if the targets given to students make sense to the student and are built into a broader framework of progression shared by students and teachers within a subject area. Progression charts for different conceptual and skills based areas within and across a key stage allow a teacher to map where their students are heading across a course and return the reader to the concept of backward planning discussed in other areas of the book. By clearly planning for progression across an AS course and into the A2 course the process of advising a student of their next steps for learning becomes easier for student and teacher. This is not to suggest students will ascend the progression chart like a ladder at an even and steady pace with a few encouraging words from their teacher along the way. Students progress at an irregular pace and strengthen in some areas of their learning before they are able to move forward in others, some students will never become adept in all areas of their subject and their will always be a range of students at different stages of competency within an AS and A2 class. If the teacher has a clear grasp of where the student is heading then this can be transferred to the students through clear and achievable targets which aim to move the student forward at a pace appropriate to their learning style. If assessment for learning is defined as: 'The process of seeking and interpreting evidence for use by learners and their teachers to decide where the learners are in their learning, where they need to go and how best to get there.' Assessment for Learning: 10 Principles Assessment Reform Group (2002), then target setting based on a subject based understanding of progression plays a crucial role in its achievement.

Targets are most effective when they are simple, clear, achievable and transferable targets, with reflection time built into lessons. Progression charts can be based upon specification assessment criteria as well as teacher's professional subject expertise. They work most effectively when discussed as a department and this can also be a starting point for developing consistency within a subject area. A comprehensive but not rigid outline of progression can be shared with students and allows students to build their own next steps as well as making target setting a much more efficient process for the teacher. Ideally such models will not be mechanistic and support the student and teacher in the learning process.

In 2003 OfSTED published a report on Good Assessment in Secondary Schools in which effective target setting was characterized by the following features:

◆ specific to the subject and relate to important aspects of knowledge, understanding and skills in that subject;
◆ derived from teacher's assessments and not only student devised.
◆ limited in number and of manageable proportions.
◆ relatively short-term, capable of being monitored and subject to regular amendment.
◆ accessible to students.
◆ drawn from or relate to, the teaching objectives of a unit of work.

To apply these goals into AS and A2 teaching is desirable and achievable. For an 'A' Level student assessment criteria and progression within a subject can be relatively narrow and as a student of fewer subjects greater time and devotion can be given by the student to meeting the targets set. An average AS student for example, will be studying four subjects or a combination of two AS's and a vocational course. Either way the issues of manageability are made easier by contact with fewer teachers and less subject variables. This enables the teacher to have a greater expectation of the student's ability to devote time to the meeting of targets and increases the role targets play in moving a student's learning forward.

Targets can be set in a variety of ways and returning to the work of Shirley Clarke, she suggests the following approaches:

Example prompts: These are clearly defined targets which show a model of the intended outcome and then ask the student to do their own, for example:

◆ Count how many breaths Karen takes between strokes and repeat in your own front crawl . . .;
◆ Read the sentences below and choose one to start your conclusion . . .;
◆ Read James' introduction, how has he gained the readers attention so quickly? Rewrite your introduction using a similar technique . . .

Scaffolded prompts: These advise a student on how to structure an area of their work more effectively to improve it further, for example:

◆ How could you use X, Y, Z to explain this point further . . .?
◆ Make use of the connectives mat to link your paragraphs more effectively . . .
◆ Rewrite your opening sentences in order to signpost your paragraphs . . .
◆ Choose an example from each of the units studied to give the piece breadth . . .

Reminder prompt: These act as an aide memoir for something a student could have done but overlooked or disregarded, for example:

◆ Explain why you think . . .;
◆ What evidence do you have to support this . . .?;
◆ Where else is this applicable . . .?;
◆ Explain this point with more subject specific vocabulary . . .

Each of the targets has a common approach. They each ask the student to do a specific action or task to improve their work immediately.

1. The student is encouraged to return to their original work.
2. The student reflects upon their original work.
3. The student looks to additional information in the form of an exemplar or further reading.
4. The student improves their work immediately based on all of the above.
5. The student resubmits their work for checking or approval.

This work is then acknowledged or marked a second time by the teacher to look for improvement. If the improvement is made the work can be praised and it would be beneficial to ask the student to reflect upon what they did to make the step forward and consider what they will need to do next time they are faced with a similar task. The target then becomes transferable, the student will hopefully recognize that they need to again employ the improvement strategy and produce an improved piece of work which will be ready for another next steps comment.

Not all students will initially be able to use targets in this way and as with other assessment for learning strategies they will need reinforcing by the teacher on a regular basis in order that the student becomes familiar with this style of working. This will require teacher and student discipline and a simple target log sheet at the front of a student planner can assist with the process. This can contain columns for the target set, a date to mark completion, a comment on how the target was addressed, a reflection on the teacher's subsequent feedback and where this feedback was reapplied at a later stage of learning.

A by-product of this approach to target setting is that students are forced to revisit previous work in order to improve the next stage of learning. A student who has difficulty with organization and forgets to file work or even keep it will struggle to make the necessary improvements. If encouraged to reflect upon this most students will begin to see relevance in maintaining an organized folder and place value on both your comments and the need to refer back to their previous work. It is immensely rewarding and motivational for a teacher to observe students valuing, responding to and making progress as a result of their student feedback. Through adopting the routines and precision of feedback and targets suggested this is possible to do.

Summary

Without feedback students cannot make the progress they deserve. Feedback can be given in lessons, on the playing field, in the laboratory and it does not have to be in response to a marked piece of work. Marking can be overwhelming and it is important to your well being that the marking load does not become unmanageable. Select key pieces only to mark, employ a range of strategies for checking other work and make time to talk to your class in order to feedback orally. Encourage student reflection of feedback and acknowledge their attempts to improve their work; this is motivating for the student and importantly for you, their teacher.

17. Peer-assessment and self-assessment

Self-assessment by pupils, far from being a luxury, is in fact an essential component of formative assessment.

Inside the Black Box, *Black and Wiliam*

Self-assessment is essential to learning because students can only achieve a learning goal if they understand that goal and can assess what they need to do to reach it.

D. R. Sadler 1989

If the aim of this chapter is to demonstrate ways of encouraging AS and A2 students to become more reflective about their learning peer- and self-assessment is integral to achieving this goal. Similarly if as teachers we wish to develop our students' ability to become independent learners they will need to be 'able to engage in self-reflection and to identify the next steps to their learning.' (Assessment Reform Group, 2002). Students are more likely to make progress if they understand what their learning intentions are and what they need to do to meet them. So far we have discussed ways in which the teacher can drive this process for the students; this section will consider how the responsibility can be shared with the students to create a partnership of shared ownership of identifying where the student is currently at in their subject understanding and what they need to do get better.

Peer assessment provides pupils with opportunities to be involved in the process of assessment and to engage in questioning, marking and feedback and be a more active participant within their own learning environment. Self-assessment takes this process a stage further by asking a student to be inward looking and self-reflective of their own achievements, successes and areas of improvement. This is a challenge for any learner irrespective of age and highly demanding for a 16–18-year old who will be dealing with a set of physiological, social and emotional self-awareness related issues. This section will consider the benefits of peer- and self-assessment and strategies that can be employed to make it a powerful assessment for learning tool and a life-long skill.

Benefits of Peer- and Self-Assessment

Peer- and self assessment is a process which requires training and practice, based upon an agreed set of criteria. It is a developmental process which requires sensitivity and rigid protocols in order for every student to benefit from it. The benefits are immense and considered in more detail below.

- *Actively engages students in learning goals*: If the student is expected to respond to learning objectives in another student's work they will be able to have a greater understanding of them. Through consideration of to what extent another student has met with learning criteria the same student may eventually be able to identify those qualities and gaps in their own learning and act accordingly to reach their target grade or beyond.
- *Clarifies learning goals and task criteria for student and teacher*: In order for a student to peer assess they must have clarity in their understanding of the learning goals. Moreover the teacher must also have clarity of the learning goals and criteria in order to share them with the students. If a student is asked to peer assess a written piece of work are you asking them to identify learning beyond knowledge and understanding. Whilst there may be a check list of content and data required within the criteria, there has to be a learning goal beyond that of content. What is it? How will it be expressed to the students? Will the task being peer marked allow for differentiation either by task or by outcome? Unless the teacher defines these areas in advance of the lesson there can be no learning. If a student does not understand the learning goals they will be unable to peer assess and the teacher will be alerted to the marker's needs as well as the needs of the student being marked.
- *Sets clear and achievable targets*: Once students become more sophisticated at peer marking and are familiar with their teacher's style of target setting, students will be able to set targets in their own language. Often such targets reflect a clearer vocabulary than teacher written targets and are more achievable. Sometimes the teacher's assistance will be required to phrase the target and the dialogue which occurs through this process can reveal areas of understanding and gaps in learning that may otherwise have been missed.
- *Builds self-esteem*: Students who become adept in this area gain a huge boost to their self-esteem as their purpose in the classroom has gone beyond that of learner. The student is an active participant in the functions of the processes of the lesson and has taken in some part the role of teacher. This is an empowering position and can help the student believe that they are mastering their subject.

◆ *Develops teacher-student and student-student rapport*: Classroom talk at 'A' Level can promote learning in many ways as discussed in Chapter One and Section 14. Peer marking encourages active dialogue between students and between teacher and student(s). Discussion is focused upon the merits and weaknesses of a student's work not on the content of the subject or on the student as a person. Relationships with a class are built through hard work and mutual respect, offering responsibility to the student's for their own learning will engender both these traits. It becomes a healthy subject focused conversation about how to improve in a given area of a subject. The more the specific the criteria are for the task the greater the level of cognitive precision there will in the conversation.

◆ *Encourages independence*: A student who can reflect upon their own work prior to handing it in for marking and feedback and identify its merits as well as the areas that further guidance or support is required in, is a student worthy of being labelled independent. Peer-and self-assessment can develop this critical awareness and are an attribute of an AS or A2 learner. (See Chapter Two for more details.)

A Calendar for peer- and self-assessment

Over the course of an academic year a student can become skilled at the processes of peer marking and reap rewards from the outcomes but a step-by-step approach such as the one mapped in the peer marking calendar (Table 3.2) is to be encouraged. This is based upon a typical AS group who will sit their examination in June. If the group are sitting an examination in January, a rethinking of timescales and pace of peer marking will be required. Similarly if it you are taking an A2 group for the first time, consult with their AS teacher as to how far they progressed with peer marking and begin from where they finished at AS, there is little to be gained by the teacher or student in starting the process from the beginning again.

On their first attempt at peer marking students will often focus on the appearance of the work, its length and presentation but rarely the actual learning criteria. This is understandable as students will feel uncomfortable critiquing another student's work and will not really know, in the first instance, what they are looking for. Personalize the

Table 3.2 Peer marking calendar

Month	Peer marking activity	Purpose
September	Ask students to look over each other's notes based on a simple three part criteria of; layout, use of keywords, legibility and feedback. Agree protocols for peer marking based on this first experience. This is important for establishing ownership of the process and inter-personal relationships	A non-threatening first activity will introduce students to peer marking. Working through the process allows the class to agree protocols, for example, discuss the work not the author; begin feedback with a positive remark
October	With target grades established and peer relationships formed introduce a 'marking buddy' system to be used with all future peer marking. Mark a class based piece of work using pre-determined subject criteria not generic skills; identify success only	'Marking buddies' help students become familiar with each other's work and confidence can grow in relation to understanding of the buddy's strengths and weaknesses. Similar ability students can work together to support or extend as necessary
November	Buddies mark a homework task using a criteria grid (this lists the task criteria and has a 'Yes' and 'No' box next to it with space for comments). Highlight areas of the work which meet the criteria successfully and indicate one area of the work which does not meet the criteria with a statement as to why it does not meet it	The criteria grid ensures a student focuses on specified areas of the work and ignores everything else. Confidence is being built though positive praise and the buddy is becoming familiar with his/her partner's style of work. There is no expectation for target setting at this point

(Continued)

Table 3.2 (*Continued*)

Month	Peer marking activity	Purpose
December	Conduct another piece of marking using a criteria grid. Set a target for the area for development and feedback to the buddy immediately. Plan time for the target to be acted upon and then debrief the quality of the target based on students' attempts to achieve it. The teacher will still be checking peer marking at this stage	This is the first attempt at target setting and buddies can base their suggestion on previous targets set by their teacher. By acting on the target immediately and then debriefing the activity the targets can be quality assured and exemplars used as a model for future target setting
January	Increase the frequency of peer marking and reduce the teacher checking based on individual pair's competencies. Use for small aspects of work rather than whole pieces to develop a range of opportunities, for example an introduction, an experiment write up, an essay plan	By reducing the teacher input greater responsibility is being passed to the students thus raising their level of independence while maintaining the security of the buddy system. Little and often can also work better within the framework of a whole lesson
February	Move to acknowledgement marking only of peer marked work. Withdraw the use of criteria grids if appropriate. Teacher will mark responses to targets	This is a consolidation period before moving onto self-assessment.

March	Using a criteria grid self-assess a piece of work of the student's choosing. Link directly to target grades and what the student needs to do to meet or exceed their expected target	Exams are approaching and the student will benefit from directly linking their work to mark schemes ad grade criteria. Self-assessment at this stage will place the student firmly in control of their own learning with support from their marking buddy and teacher as and when it is required
April	Combine regular use of peer- and self-assessment in relation to examination assessment objectives. Link individual target setting to revision schedules.	Examination preparations will now be taking priority and revision schedules can be built around next step targets from previously peer and self assessed work. This aims to engage the student directly with their exam preparation rather than it being imposed by the teacher
May	Regularly mark and feedback on exam practice using examiner's reports and examination mark schemes	Encourages prompt feedback within minutes of completing a question, familiarizes students with exam mark schemes and criteria.

plan to the needs of the individual group of students; it will be different every year.

Strategies for peer- and self-assessment

The calendar suggests a range of peer- and self-assessment strategies which require greater consideration. Below are the calendar strategies in greater depth and a few alternative strategies to help 'A' Level students become more proficient in this skill.

- *Marking buddies*: By creating marking partnerships students will be able to forge a relationship of trust and support with a classmate and use them like a teacher would use a mentor or coach. By waiting to establish the partnerships the teacher will have a more informed understanding of each student's strengths, social skills, friendships and can pair students with due consideration of all these factors. It would be wise to allow students to speak to you privately if at any point they are uncomfortable with their marking buddy but where possible try to avoid swapping as the students have to view this as a professional as well as personal relationship. The benefits of placing similar ability students together are discussed in Chapters One and Four and placing an 'E' grade student with an 'A' grade student would beg the question 'Who is gaining for the partnership?'
- *Random selection*: In order to ensure that students are exposed to a wide variety of styles and approaches to a task there is merit in randomly redistributing work rather than orchestrating who marks who. However 'A' Level students very quickly become aware of each other's style and the anonymity of marking in this way does not last for long. At post-16 a more mature and consistent approach to peer marking may be appropriate.
- *Use of criteria*: Most studies of peer- and self-assessment will support the belief that it can only be effectual when accompanied by clearly defined criteria. This criteria can be based upon external examination objectives or be smaller task-specific criteria. It may be accompanied by a level or grade or may simply be on a can/ cannot do basis. There is no suggestion of a preferred system simply that there must be shared and defined criteria for the peer-assessment to be effectual.
- *Regular and staged*: Students will find peer-assessment challenging on the first occasions just as teachers found their first ever set of

'A' Level marking daunting and terrifying. Minimize the expectation by using a staged approach to peer- and self-assessment at a pace that works for the group and the individuals within the group. As with other reflective learning strategies it benefits for being planned for within the short and medium term and lesson time will need to be afforded to it on a regular basis if it to be successful. An attempt here and there will waste teacher and learner time and make little or no impact on student learning. As a teacher you will need to commit yourself to the immense benefits of peer- and self-assessment and be prepared for limited success to begin with.

◆ *Model previous work*: A non-threatening entry into peer marking is through the use of previous student's work and modelling of a peer marking activity. Using a range of work by previous students enables peer markers to be honest about work without the anxiety that the author is in the room or at next to them. This is an effective method to employ if you are trying to speed up the pace of peer marking or if you need to move student on more quickly. It can also be a useful exercise to undertake each time the class embarks upon a more challenging aspect of peer or self marking to reassure the marker and build student confidence.

◆ *Amend promptly*: Already discussed in Section 15 but worth reinforcing, allow time for feeding forward from peer feedback as you would do for teacher led feedback.

◆ *Viva*: This is a common technique used at university to discuss an undergraduates' work and their level of understanding in a particular field. It is often used when a student is a borderline class of degree and the lecture wishes to determine the degree they should receive. In an 'A' Level lesson a similar approach can be used between marking buddies or between a small group of students. Rather than a marking buddy reading and assessing a student's work, the author or creator of the work presents it to the marking buddy and explains what they did and how they have reached particular findings or conclusions. The marking buddy then peer marks in a familiar way. This approach has two clear benefits: first the presenter of the work has to have an understanding of what they have done and they cannot bluff or plagiarize. Second the dialogue which occurs between the students is consolidation of prior leaning and allows the students to explore further themes and ideas presented through the work. As the teacher you can listen into their conversation and form your own judgement about student learning and plan next steps accordingly.

All of these strategies put the student at the centre of assessment. It is a course of action they are part of not a victim to. Whether used formatively or summatively peer- and self-assessment are foremost, revealing about the strengths and needs of a student and engages them in the learning and assessment process.

Summary

Peer-assessment has many beneficiaries. The student gains an 'insider's' view of the assessment and learning process which they can put to effective use in their own work. The teacher finds that his/her students are more receptive to feedback and often make progress at an increased rate. The teacher will also find a diminished marking load in the long term as their students become more adept and rigorous at the marking process. The overall winner is the class as a whole, who form a collaborative and supportive working relationship and understand the relative strengths and targets of each member of the class. When planned for and strategically introduced the benefits are greater than the final examination grade.

18. Preparing for the final examination

Most of the discussion so far has been in relation to formative assessment and encouraging students to become more independent and reflective learners. External examination is the final measure of a student's ability. This final section will consider methods of preparing students for the final examination through a range of teaching and learning strategies that maintain student involvement and equip them with the necessary skills to achieve their potential in their final examination. These are not techniques that teach to the examination or enable students to functionally jump through the necessary hoops, merely a range of methods to prepare students for the examination and retain their identity as scholars. All the suggestions can be applied to any examination at AS and A2 and can be used throughout the taught course, not just in the revision phase of the curriculum. Chapter Five deals with revision techniques in and out of the classroom and there is overlap across this section and the Chapter Five.

♦ *Exam familiarization*: From the very beginning of a course it is helpful to show students a final examination in order that they can familiarize themselves with what and how they will be finally assessed. At AS this can be an uplifting process as it removes the fear factor of the final examination and alerts them to next stage in education. Often the question style will bear a resemblance to GCSE as will the assessment objectives thus removing the mystery of the final examination. Although the content knowledge will be absent at the start of the course, acquaintance with the final goal post can be reassuring for future learning.

♦ *Exam practice*: Chapter One deals with strategies for teaching and learning which move the learner away from examination style questions. It is still important however to make use of examination papers on a regular basis and make formative use of their results. The key is to use them regularly but infrequently in order that they do not dominate the teaching schedule. Responses can be planned together and peer assessed or used as a consolidation activity at the end of a sequence of lessons.

♦ *Examiners reports and mark schemes*: This is another exercise designed to demystify the examination process. Students are often unaware of an examiner's wish to mark positively and reward achievement wherever possible. Examiners' reports often contain guidance on how to tackle certain aspects of an examination paper and offer 'top tips' to help teachers equip their students with the necessary learning tools. Marks schemes will also contain suggested content appropriate to a specific question and when used as a debriefing exercise to a particular question or topic can be reassuring for students.

♦ *Devise own papers or mark schemes*: Once familiar with an examination and its mark scheme students can engage in writing their own examination papers or mark schemes. This activity can be made purposeful by actually using the papers for their or another class. By preparing a question students have to consider which question style can access the relevant assessment objectives. Similarly preparing a mark scheme will challenge students to unpick an assessment objective and the progression within it. Students can then incorporate their ideas into their own responses. The extent to which students cope with this activity will provide the teacher with formative information about the individuals in their class.

◆ *Plan together*: This is reassuring for all students and can extend the thinking of a more-able student. Planning answers is to be encouraged in all subjects and when incorporated into everyday lessons students will become familiar with the practices and benefits of it. Set strict time limits as the examination approaches in order that students can apply the skill of planning in the final examination rather than see it as a luxury that cannot be afforded in a timed environment.

◆ *Model*: Many Sixth Form colleges and centres take advantage of the examination board facility to recall papers. This is immensely useful when trying to gauge exactly what the examiners were looking for and what constitutes an A, C, E grade. Teachers often use these papers as part of the professional development but fewer share them with the students. There are ethical issues regarding names on papers and scripts must be made anonymous. Make use of 'real papers' when modelling a response or introducing peer marking strategies. Students are often willing to be more critical of anonymous work and will be heartened by what a 'C' grade looks like.

◆ *Practice timing*: This is one of the most common hurdles in a final examination and students can poorly time their responses and not achieve the grade they deserve. As the examination approaches reduce the time students have to prepare, plan and execute a response in order that the final examination feels like a classroom activity.

Through formative use of the outcomes of these activities students are being provided with the opportunity to prepare for the examination and a reflective understanding of what they will need to do to secure the very best grade they can, raising educational standards for all students.

Summary

Examination preparation and an understanding of how the final summative examination will appear is a necessary part of 'A' Level teaching and learning. It is important to use this as an aspect of the teaching and learning strategies not the driving force of all lessons. Pressure on teachers to achieve results can place an unnecessary emphasis upon examination practice. Use it when necessary, regularly revisit examination papers but do not let the examination dominate the classroom. When they are being used try to incorporate formative assessment techniques and enlivened ways of approaching them to maintain your captivating classroom.

Chapter summary

Knowing your students and building a positive working relationship with them takes an investment of time and energy. Yet it is these relationships that shape you as a teacher and influence the way you plan, think and work. Students will give everything for a teacher who they believe cares about them and their work. Teaching students to be reflective develops from these relationships and students being able to employ the same care and attention to their learning that you give to theirs. Helping students make progress is not based on grades and levels it is based on their understanding of the subject and how to progress within it. By making use of all or some of the suggested strategies you will gain a better understanding of the students you teach and in turn they will appreciate their own learning more successfully.

4 | Extending students' thinking

As 'a rising tide lifts all ships', Gifted and Talented education can raise the aspirations, achievements, motivation and self-esteem of all pupils.
Neil McIntosh, CfBT 2007

There is a lot of material for pre-16s and it seems to be assumed that it can be adapted to suit older learners. Post-16 provision seems to be treated as something of a bolt-on or afterthought.
Mike Bulmer, Aimhigher

Gifted and talented education remains one of the most contentious areas of the current England and Wales' comprehensive education agenda. 'Its elitist!' was not an uncommon cry in many staffrooms when Gifted and Talented (G&T) issues were initially raised. Gradually through the inclusion agenda and the move towards a more personalized curriculum the G&T agenda has risen in profile within schools. Similarly in many local authorities and institutions, programmes are in place to meet the needs of 11–16 learners.

Research and theory surrounding the area of G&T education is plentiful. The DCSF and other agencies have invested time and resources into ensuring support materials and personnel are available to help school leaders and teachers move forward in their understanding and practice of G&T teaching and learning. Unfortunately, development and practice in post-16 G&T education is less well-documented and colleges and Sixth Forms are implementing their own programmes at their own pace depending upon enthusiasm of individual leaders and teachers alongside pressure from other interested groups and stakeholders.

This chapter aims to explore post-16 educational theory and pedagogic practice in G&T education. It will also endeavour to show that every lesson and learning activity can aspire to meet the needs of the most able AS and A2 students. As in previous chapters the emphasis will be on practical learning strategies and applying a range of techniques to different subject areas. More than any other area of the book, this chapter will directly respond to what students have said about how they wish to learn in a challenging educational environment.

19. Who are G&T students at 'A' Level?

The goal is that five years from now; gifted and talented students progress in line with their ability rather than their age; schools inform parents about tailored provision in an annual school profile; curricula include a gifted and talented dimension and at 14–19 there is more stretch and differentiation at the top end, so no matter what your talent it will be engaged; and the effect of poverty on achievement is reduced, because support for higher ability students from poorer backgrounds enables them to thrive.

Speech at National Academy for Gifted and Talented Youth – David Miliband, Minister of State for School Standards, May 2004

What does it mean to be 'gifted and talented'?

The DCSF/CfBT Young Gifted and Talented programme defines G&T learners aged 11–19 as 'those pupils who would fall into the national top 5 per cent by ability and other pupils who are gifted and talented, relative to their peers in their own year group in their school'. The National Association of Children Exceptional (NACE) does not offer a discreet definition of G&T and instead offers 'support for teachers in getting the best from able, gifted and talented pupils in the everyday classroom, whilst enabling all pupils to flourish'. The DCSF spend the largest section of their guidance document 'Effective Provision for Gifted and Talented Students in Secondary Education', advising schools how to develop their own identification policy and define their own identification criteria.

Schools are encouraged to make use of various forms of data to identify their G&T population, examples of which include DCSF Key to Success data, results from examinations at the end of each key stage and other external qualifications. Teachers and other adults are encouraged to engage in the identification process to ensure a move away from a purely academic G&T cohort and ensure 'Talent' plays as important a role as 'Giftedness' in the make up of a whole school G&T register.

In January 2008 it was reported in the CfBT National Register Annual Report based on School Census statistics, that 92 per cent of secondary schools identify their G&T pupils resulting in a national primary and secondary register of 780,250 pupils. In statistical terms schools are advised that a G&T cohort will be between 10–20 per cent of the school population but will vary, depending upon the diversity of the student intake. In the aforementioned report of January 2008, 11.8 per cent of secondary students are identified as G&T. In post-16 education this cohort will be multi-dimensional and will not fit a nominal percentage medium. Commonly post-16 institutions will base their register on the principal criteria of a 7+ average GCSE points score on entry. Increasingly however there will be vocational G&T learners whose end destination may not be university. Regionally and nationally recognized sportsmen and women may not achieve a high point score average but their athletic ability will require appreciation, nurture and support from their educational institution especially in periods of critical competition and arduous training schedules. Identification at post-16 therefore does not become 'easier' as the spotlight shines on the academically bright; it becomes increasingly diverse and non-stereotypical and colleges and Sixth Forms will need to ensure a fluid and regularly reworked register to ensure maximum identification of student needs.

Whole college identification procedures and programmes are largely out of the hands of individual teachers and it is the role of each post-16 teacher to make use of the identification procedures, in order to be attentive to the needs of all their students including the most-able. Teachers should be making use of the entry data of each student in order to begin the identification procedure and be vigilant to the indicators of outstanding ability as and when they begin to emerge. Teachers who lack confidence or expertise in this area need to be willing to ask for and be offered support from department and school colleagues in this field. Only then can the strategies suggested in subsequent sections of this chapter be successfully employed and benefited from.

20. G&T students and their individual needs

Many people believe that 'giftedness will out' but research shows that this is not true and that giftedness needs to be 'coaxed out' through access to challenging opportunities, appropriate help and guidance.
www.warwick.ac.uk/gifted

General principles for thinking about G&T provision are coherently laid out in the DCSF document 'Guidance on Effective Provision for

Gifted and Talented Students in Secondary Education' coordinated by Professor Deborah Eyre, former Director of the National Academy for Gifted and Talented Youth. The document recommends readers to consider their exit point for students when embarking upon G&T provision. Eyre suggests teachers ask the question, 'What do you want to have achieved for these students prior to their move to post-school destinations?' This open ended question encourages teachers to again reflect upon where they want students to be at the end of their AS and A2 courses and engage in backward planning to ensure intentions are met. An individual teacher or departmental response may be narrower in focus than a whole school and college answer but it is likely that most answers will refer to a student's learning and emotional behaviours in addition to their examinable and non-examinable achievement. The guidance attempts to provide insight into how these overarching aims can be met and the key points to how to achieve success in 11–19 G&T provision are summarized below. These are also the five components of the personalized learning agenda.

Effective teaching and learning strategies

- ◆ Excellent teaching with reference to the classroom quality standards.
- ◆ The learning environment.
- ◆ Task planning.
- ◆ Questioning.
- ◆ Individual young people.
- ◆ Self-esteem and motivation.
- ◆ Enabling curriculum entitlement and choice.
- ◆ Assessment for learning.
- ◆ Organizing the school.
- ◆ Strong partnerships beyond the school.

Organizing the school, enabling curriculum entitlement and choice and strong partnerships beyond the school are largely beyond an individual teacher's control but other areas of effective teaching and learning strategies and assessment for learning are widely agreed to be the bedrock of successful pedagogic practice. In turn G&T students are identifying these two areas as the critical pre-requisites for engaging learning. G&T Update published the findings of one student's thoughts on 'What makes a good teacher for gifted and talented students?' (G&T Update month 2007) The student noted that a good teacher would attempt to ensure all of the following:

◆ enjoyment in the topic and activity;
◆ provided work which stretched a student's thinking;
◆ made use of appropriate learning styles to challenge student comfort zones (see Chapter One);
◆ issued different homework assignments (see Chapter Two);
◆ set higher but realistic targets (see Chapter Three).

Whilst this is a commendable checklist, its contents are arguably applicable to the teaching of all students, not just those who are deemed gifted or talented. A series of interviews with post-16 students in Norfolk offered a more defined selection of criteria for effective teaching.

G&T student comments on effective teaching

◆ Activities are challenging.
◆ Questions are presented as problems to solve.
◆ Work is personalized and not the same for all students.
◆ Content deviates from the curriculum and animates the teacher.
◆ Links between and across topics are looked for.
◆ Feedback is prompt and personal.
◆ Work has a point and purpose.

This list is more challenging to a teacher as it requires a teacher to question what they are teaching; why they are teaching it and how they are going to engage the most-able learners into the lesson. Lesson objectives can be driven by the criteria mapped by the students and Section 21 will explore the means by which objectives can be achieved. The Norfolk students' comments are further endorsed by a manifesto produced by post-16 students at a Villiers

Park Education Trust Conference in 2007. Villiers Park Educational Trust has been working with able post-16 students for 40 years and over 10,000 have attended residential courses at their centres. The students come from all types of schools and colleges and from across UK. In addition to in-house events they run a wide range of day long master classes at universities nationwide. They construct most of their course as a result of listening to what the students say and what works in practice. The students' comments are printed below.

Villiers Park Education Trust student manifesto on 'what makes outstanding learning experiences'

◆ Strong mutual student-teacher relationships.
◆ Appreciation of individual learning styles.
◆ One-to-one student teacher consultation.
◆ Optimized use of lesson time.
◆ Relevant trips and visits.
◆ Up-to-date resources with home access to online learning.
◆ Links to outside agencies.

Collectively these student voiced comments, provide teachers with clear guidance on what and how to teach G&T students. They desire personalized learning in its literal sense of being personal to their individual learning needs. Christine Gilbert in the DCSF 2020 Vision paper describes personalization as a 'highly structured and responsive approach'. At its conception personalization was confused with individualization, where children work individually or are left to their own devices. On the contrary personalized learning is designed to respond to the learning needs of individual students in their own school or college. At the heart of personalized learning is assessment for learning, the most critical tool in developing and personalizing learning for the gifted and talented. In the teaching of the most-able, lessons which try to incorporate as many of the student-driven effective learning criteria as possible will enable the teacher to have a purposeful understanding of the individual's learning needs. What this actually looks like in or out of a classroom will be explored in Section 21.

Summary

You will need to remain alert to your own college or school's identification procedures and G&T register in order to be alert to students in your class who have the potential to be the most-able learners. Departmental criteria and registers will make the process more pertinent to your subject area and allow you to monitor the progress of the potentially able. Consider the student voice checklists in context of your own lesson and how many of the desired facets of teaching and learning take place within your own lesson. Discuss these criteria with a colleague or as a whole department and share examples of practice where the criteria have been met. This is a challenging area of teaching and most schools and colleges should have a G&T coordinator or leading teacher who will be able to offer advice and support.

21. G&T learning in the classroom

The most central need is for gifted children to be stretched. This does not mean working faster, or doing more of the same. Rather, it means engaging in a higher quality and more stimulating course of work.

Chris Kyriacou, Effective Teaching in Schools, 1997

Classroom quality standards

The plethora of research on teaching more-able children has been put to practical use through the publication of the Institutional Quality Standards and the Classroom Quality Standards by the DCSF. Devised in conjunction with NAGTY, DCSF and other interest groups, they are a set of levelled criteria to help schools identify whether their G&T provision is at entry, developing or exemplary level. They are organized under five headings designed to overlap with the personalized learning agenda discussed earlier in Section 20 and in Chapter Three. They are initially designed to be used by G&T coordinators and school leaders and offer limited use to a classroom teacher. To overcome this drawback, 2007 saw the publication of the Classroom

Quality Standards. This excellent document provides the teacher with a more teaching and learning specific tool to assess the level of provision for gifted and talented taking place within a classroom and thus in every day lessons. These standards are again at entry, developing and exemplary level and are organized under the following headings:

◆ Conditions for Learning.
◆ Development of Learning.
◆ Knowledge of Subjects and Themes.
◆ Understanding Learners Needs.
◆ Planning.
◆ Engagement with Learners and Learning.
◆ Links Beyond the Classroom.

These headings provide an instructional tool for any teacher of any ability but they can be easily transferred to the needs of an 'A' Level classroom and the more-able students within what is often a very mixed-ability environment. Whilst designed as an audit tool they can be a helpful prompt as to how to address the needs of more-able learners through the opportunity for next steps planning. For example, at the entry level of Knowledge of Subjects and Themes, under the prompt: How well is learning developed through specific subject knowledge and skills. Exemplary practice will possess the following qualities:

> *Clear progressions and connections between subjects are identified and adapted to G&T learners' needs and interests. G&T learners have frequent opportunity to demonstrate expert application of specific skills and knowledge, and this is supported through excellent coaching.*

Although wordy there are some excellent suggestions within this phrase for teaching the more-able student. First, cross curricular learning and links are encouraged to enhance the demands of a specific subject. Second, the teacher helps the student to identify the links and then connects with the individual student's areas of interest thus making connections for this student rather than any student. Third, the student is being encouraged to apply their specific learning within a range of teacher-created opportunities, through application the student can demonstrate their learning and improve upon their performance. Finally the teacher is supporting the student through coaching thus encouraging an independent learner and further advancing the student through facilitating their development as an independent learner. There are 18 more exemplary standards all as helpful and aspirational as this one. It is helpful to complete the audit before embarking upon the standards to help a teacher make one improvement at a time – they can be a bit overwhelming otherwise.

Do's and don'ts

Section 20 refers to students' voice and what students regard as effective and engaging teaching and learning. Table 4.1 titled 'Do's and Don'ts Student Voice' provides a detailed summary of students' comments in relation to their thoughts on effective planning, teaching and learning strategies and learning outside of the classroom. The awareness that post-16 students display in regard to the different

Table 4.1   'Do's and Don'ts' – Student voice

Norfolk student voice/ Villiers Park student conference	Teachers 'please do . . .'	Teachers 'please do not . . .'
Planning	◆ Demonstrate links across learning in KS3-GCSE-AS-A2 ◆ Incorporate independent learning ◆ Plan work outside the 'comfort zone' ◆ Let students help plan ◆ Plan with an appreciation of individual learning styles ◆ Optimize use of lesson time	◆ Pitch to the middle ◆ Give more of the same ◆ Make assumptions about prior learning ◆ Repeat learning ◆ Force opinions ◆ Create unnecessary pressure and stress through unreasonable homework and coursework deadlines

(*Continued*)

Table 4.1 (*Cont'd*)

Norfolk student voice/Villiers Park student conference	Teachers 'please do . . .'	Teachers 'please do not. . .'
	◆ Make students aware of syllabus and long-term learning objectives ◆ Plan for opportunities to work with similarly motivated students	
Strategies	◆ Regular analysis of methods of working ◆ Debate in role – avoid stereotypes ◆ Create own assessment with response criteria ◆ Writing in different genre and for a different audience ◆ Make use of music in all subject areas ◆ Problem-solving activities ◆ Offer a variety of lesson styles ◆ Let students create a starter or run the plenary	◆ Delay feedback ◆ Make homework a repetition of prior learning ◆ Ignore those consistently achieving ◆ Be unenthusiastic ◆ Spoon-feed
Outside the classroom	◆ Have educational trips to provide new experience and the opportunity to meet new people ◆ Ensure an accessible wide range of up-to-date resources with access at home to online parts	◆ Have a lack of cohesion in the timetable ◆ Place too much emphasis on key skills and general studies

aspects of learning demonstrates the importance they place on the complex number of facets which make up their learning experience. Planning for learning is regarded with a respect that a younger or less-able student would struggle to identify. The strategies used to deliver this planning are placed at the heart of their learning experience and interest is given by the students to how their learning can be further developed once they leave the classroom. The common denominator for all their suggestions is the desire to extend students' thinking and involvement with each aspect of the learning process. There now follows greater exploration and explanation of a selection of their ideas, while others are enhanced and extended.

Planning

◆ *Demonstrate links across learning in KS3-GCSE-AS-A2*: Students want to make connections across their learning. By encouraging G&T students to identify links from prior learning to the current area of study the level of thinking and challenge are immediately increased. In the 1950s Benjamin Bloom and associates devised a ranking to reflect the level of challenge present within different types of questions and activities. This is commonly known as Bloom's taxonomy and moves students from knowledge, comprehension and application focused questions and tasks to higher order thinking skills of analysis, synthesis and evaluation. Synthesis requires students to combine old ideas to create new ones and to generalize from previous knowledge. Exploring more-able students' prior learning and challenging them to combine, integrate, modify, rearrange, substitute, plan, design, invent, compose, formulate, prepare, generalize or rewrite in relation to a new area of learning will push them beyond their regular 'comfort zone'.

In practice this could be applied to a chemistry lesson. Part of the AS syllabus for OCR is chains, energy and resources – topics which will have been covered at a more basic level though the KS3 SAT and GCSE. More-able students will quickly become disengaged with repetition of learning but making use of their expertise and prior learning will increase confidence and create a high level of expectation within the lesson. Allow the more-able to use their prior learning to create a hypothesis linked to hydrocarbons and define their own practical experiment to prove/disprove their theory.

◆ *Incorporate independent learning*: Chapter Two covers this area in detail and independent learning techniques are often used with the more-able learners as previously discussed. The freedom to plan their own learning, outcomes and time frames can be particularly appealing to the more-able learner and encourage the student to reflect upon the method of their learning rather than simply letting them do the task that is required of them, will prove interesting and stimulating. At the apex of Bloom's taxonomy lies evaluation which requires students to assess, decide, rank, grade, measure, recommend, convince, select, judge, discriminate, support, conclude and summarize. Independent learning can demand all these applications in terms of subject work and in analysing method of working.

◆ *Plan work outside the 'comfort zone'*: This is a by-product of using the techniques discussed yet it is interesting that more-able students want to be challenged to work in this way. By moving away from familiar techniques and strategies for learning they are being forced to adapt their learning to new techniques as well as question the way they work and confront their own secure approaches to learning and subject understanding.

◆ *Let students help plan*: This sounds quite dangerous in an AS and A2 learning environment. Is it appropriate to involve students in a pre-determined course and how will colleagues' respond to such a potentially risky endeavour? The important aspect of this strategy is to remember the teacher is planning with G&T students in mind, not the whole class. G&T students like to see the big picture of their learning and where the course is taking them and how it fits with previous and other study. An extra assignment for the G&T students could be to involve them in the planning of a given aspect of the syllabus or course. Ask the students questions such as:

  ◇ How would you approach this topic?
  ◇ What prior learning is required to appreciate this unit?
  ◇ Which resources will be most useful in the study of this area?
  ◇ Is there a field trip that would enhance the topic or skill involved?

Through asking G&T students similar questions and others analysis type questions designed to promote the students' ability to see patterns or identify components of learning a higher level of thinking will be induced.

◆ *Plan with an appreciation of individual learning styles*: There is an array of contemporary research into the merits and demerits of different learning styles. It is purported (and countered) that visual, auditory and kinaesthetic learners respond to learning in different ways and find it demanding to work in an alternative learning style. Encouraging G&T students to identify different learning styles and consider which can work more effectively than others for different types of learning can be stretching and have long-term benefit when they are working independently or revising. If they are able to make an informed decision regarding which learning styles to employ when revising different subjects, and goes beyond being simply helpful, it will also apply in future academic, vocational or professional life.

◆ *Optimize use of lesson time*: It has already been identified in previous chapters how precious learning time can be at AS and A2. The benefits of medium-term planning to ensure adequate coverage of the syllabus are addressed in Chapter One. For students to raise the issue of optimizing lesson time implies that some students do not always regard lesson time as being deployed in the most efficient manner to maximize learning. When every minute of each lesson does not count, the more-able student can become immensely frustrated and invariably bored. It is a test for every teacher to make every second of every lesson count and one way to achieve this is through effective planning with clearly identified and measurable lesson objectives and outcomes as well as mapped stages within a lesson to ensure students are being moved forward throughout the lesson.

◆ *Make students aware of syllabus and long-term learning objectives*: This has been partially addressed through other planning suggestions and is explored in Chapter Two. Clear learning goals and direction can provide the learning structures that all students need, G&T students can extend this knowledge further and look beyond the approved curriculum to extend and enhance the prescribed course.

◆ *Plan for opportunities to work with similarly motivated students*: It has been frequently stated in this book that 'A' Level teaching can be incredibly mixed ability. Teaching conventions and strategies have been suggested to deal with a broad range of abilities and in Chapter One the value of like-minded students working together is addressed. Conversations with G&T students have led me to draw the conclusion that able students enjoy the challenge of working with other G&T students in and out of the classroom. A more-able student can be intimidating to a less-able student and the less-able student will not pose the necessary challenge to force the more-able student into cognitive conflict or a tension in their learning. Neither student is gaining in terms of their learning. The less-able student loses confidence in the level of their own learning and the more-able student becomes over-confident or worse bored by the lack of peer challenge. A teacher should consider social and emotional aspects of teaching and learning in planning to ensure neither student is exposed to such outcomes. If G&T students enjoy the opportunity to work with like-minded students and it benefits their subject understanding it is advisable to plan for such occasions.

Strategies

◆ *Regular analysis of methods of working*: For G&T students, reflecting upon their process of thinking is crucial. It helps them develop as reflective learners and become increasingly self-aware. At AS and A2 this has multiple benefits as they mature into subject specialists and what being a student of music, science or English means in subject-specific terms and how their work can vary and improve depending on the nature of study and what is being asked of them. As Chapter Five demonstrates the greater the repertoire of learning techniques the more informed a student can be when deciding which learning strategy to employ. A G&T student may be engaged in a range of learning activities such as master classes or in college projects and informed analysis of their working methods can only enhance such accomplishments.

◆ *Debate in role, avoid stereotypes*: Classroom talk has been discussed at length in Chapter One. Encouraging students to talk in role promotes their awareness of the possible thoughts and actions of other involved individuals or groups. Such activities can unfortunately lead to stereotyping of groups of people and limit thinking rather than develop it further. A G&T student will benefit from the opportunity to debate in role but the role needs to be clearly defined by the teacher or by the student to avoid becoming one dimensional. For example, a Biology debate on cloning may include a scientist, a doctor, an individual carrying an untreatable disease and a tabloid journalist. The G&T student can be encouraged to research and build their character based on a series of real life case studies and independent research thus extending their knowledge base but also developing evaluative skills through selecting and judging the most appropriate course of thinking for their chosen individual.

◆ *Create own assessment with response criteria*: As Chapter Three explores, the use of assessment criteria is an essential tool in moving all AS and A2 students forward. For G&T students the 'scaffold can appear more of a cage' and restrict their expression and individual creativity. While G&T students need to understand how they will be examined and make use of examination criteria they can become more involved in the assessment process through developing their own response criteria. To help G&T students become more aware of what it means to study a subject and how to think in subject terms, hand the assessment responsibility over to them and ask them to consider what a top-level mark scheme and response in a specified aspect of the subject would look for and look like. Tell the student to avoid generic comments and ask them to directly focus on one specific concept or process within the subject. By creating a levelled response the student will begin to develop their own sense of progression within the subject and what it means to get better in a specific-subject area.

For example, in Religious Studies ask the more-able to prepare an examination question on religious ethics with levelled marking criteria and after the class has attempted the question use the students who prepared the question as team leaders in a peer marking exercise. This will enable the students to evaluate the scope within their question and redraft the mark scheme in light of actual responses.

◆ *Writing in different genre and for a different audience*: Adapting to different audiences is challenging for all writers. Undoubtedly some audiences are easier to write for than others. This may be because they require less analysis of subject or learning or because it is the audience the student typically writes for. At AS and A2 it can be tempting to encourage students to always write for an examination focused audience to ensure examination results are of a high standard. With limited time to prepare students for AS and A2 it can be viewed as time wasting to explore different genres of writing if they do not actively support the examination focus. On the contrary, using different genres can encourage a G&T student to pay closer attention to their choice of content, language and argument. The variety of task will encourage the student to rethink subject content and delivery in different ways and challenge their own assumptions and prior learning.

For example, a student of music will be familiar with critical and analytical writing relating to the historical study of music. They may regularly write with their teacher or future examiner in mind but they could vary their audience without losing their skills of comparison and historical analysis. Vary the audience by asking the students to prepare the insert of a CD cover critiquing the chosen music of study. Alternatively they could prepare a historical musical journey for use in a GCSE history classroom utilizing skills of selection as well as exploring change and continuity over time. Finally the students could write a pitch for an historical film maker arguing that the chosen pieces would reflect the period and required dramatic tension.

♦ *Problem-solving activities*: A large amount of AS and A2 teaching revolves around the ensuring the delivery of subject-specific content. As previously discussed, content does not need to be didactically conveyed to students and one method of achieving this is through the use of problem-solving activities. Returning to Bloom's taxonomy the higher order thinking skills of synthesis and evaluation require students to relate, predict, verify and assess their subject knowledge. This requires students to ask and answer questions based around problems which challenge their assumptions; look at the unusual or consider material from an oblique perspective. G&T students often respond to such challenges with enthusiasm. Lesson time can be spent generating ideas based on information and issues raised in class and necessitates engagement with the knowledge base without 'spoon-feeding' of facts and data. For example, a PE lesson focusing on socio-cultural studies relating to participation in physical activity could pose the following challenge: 'Using socio-cultural research write a report for the government of Australia suggesting ways to increase Aboriginal involvement in national sport?'

♦ *Offer a variety of lesson styles*: In the same way that learning styles can be varied within lessons, lesson styles can also be varied across a unit or a term. A teacher may see their A2 class three times a week and each lesson can offer a different style or format. Lesson one may be based around an independent learning technique, lesson two could follow through with an oral focus of the knowledge learned in lesson one and lesson three can consolidate learning with a final outcome in written or other form. The lessons are diverse yet have continuity from one to the other; they are not different for the sake of it but varied to ensure a range of learning opportunities and will maintain a high level of student interest, especially that of the most-able who may be able to consider why the teacher has approached the lesson sequence in their chosen manner. If you are very brave ask the students if the chosen lesson style was the most appropriate means to meet the lesson objectives.

◆ *Let students create a starter or run the plenary*: If the teacher has chosen to involve students in the lesson planning why not take it a step further and involve them in the delivery of the lesson as well. Producing a starting activity or asking them to research some initial stimulus material can engage the more-able students with the lesson purpose and develop their knowledge and understanding. By handing the plenary over to the student, plenary style questions (examples of which are listed below) have to be understood, made accessible and steered by the G&T student toward other students.

◇ What have you learned?
◇ What gaps are there in your learning?
◇ How did you learn it?
◇ Where else can your learning be applied?

This will challenge their own learning and encourage the more-able student to consider the learning of others and how they can support their peers. Teaching others is widely regarded as one of the most effective ways for an individual to learn.

Each of these strategies has several common factors. They all:

◇ encourage a student to think about what and how they are learning;
◇ focus on the questioning of knowledge, not the acquiring of it;
◇ hand over large aspects of the lesson to the student and use the teacher as a facilitator to learning;
◇ keep lessons interesting and varied.

G&T students want to be motivated and challenged, a teacher can achieve this through making use a range of the planning techniques and lesson strategies suggested.

Summary

Post-16 lessons can be personalized and meet the needs of all learners with careful thought and planning. By varying the strategies used to access and stimulate the learning within the AS and A2 course, the most-able students will be able to derive as much from lessons as their peers. Differentiate the tasks given to students to raise their level of thinking and try to think more about your subject than the final examination. This will liberate your lesson planning and involve students in the rigours of your subject discipline.

22. G&T enrichment beyond the classroom

potential + opportunities/support + motivation = high achievement
Deborah Eyre, 2003

Sixth Form centres and colleges often seek to enrich their AS and A2 students' learning experience through the use of educational visits and trips, yet evidence tends to suggest that learning outside the classroom is on the decline nationally. Partly because of this national trend, learning beyond the classroom has in recent years, raised its national profile. The Education and Skills Select Committee published its 'Learning Outside the Classroom Manifesto'(DCSF 2006) with the intention of encouraging students to work beyond the confines of the classroom and engage them in 'learning experiences of agreed high quality' in the school grounds, the local community and further a field. The current definition of learning outside the classroom has broadened beyond visits and trips and now refers to any educational experience which does not take place within the classroom. This can be characterized as anything from distance online learning to master classes and residential summer schools. G&T students interviewed endorsed the view that learning beyond the classroom can be relevant and interesting. They suggest a range of beyond the classroom activities which are again explored in greater detail below.

◆ *Use educational trips to provide relevant experience*: The fear of risks and bureaucracy have in recent years curtailed the number of teachers who are willing to embark upon and take responsibility for educational visits and trips. College staff may object to students missing lessons in an exam-dominated calendar and cost can be seen as a discriminatory factor. These are real concerns for teachers yet a sense of perspective must be maintained; is one missed lesson of one subject a fair argument against missing out on a day of being immersed in another relevant experience? Which will the student remember more: the visit or an hour of lesson in, for example, Law?

Local authorities are using online risk assessment packages such as 'Evolve' to make the visit process easier and safer for teachers and staff. Funding can be available from in-house budgets and local clubs and businesses to support students unable to finance themselves and many organizations who have signed up to the 'Manifesto' are willing to waver some costs for special circumstances.

For G&T students visits can be used to enrich and extend their curriculum opportunities and for many to raise their aspirations. One or two wisely chosen visits within a year are worth far more than several smaller, less relevant visits. An art and design course may find it more valuable to conduct a two day visit to the galleries of Paris or London than three part day visits to the local art collections. When planned as part of the taught course the event can be published on the college calendar, forewarning other teachers of impending absence as well as being highly motivational for students and staff.

◆ *The opportunity to meet new people*: In a world where young people communicate through a variety of virtual medium it is reassuring that students still value face-to-face contact with each other and with new people. To speak and work alongside like-minded people is an indicator of a maturing mind and post-16 students enjoy the intellectual and social rewards such activities bring. This can be achieved at a local level through pairing up with a local school, club or society or on a regional or national scale through the use of specific programmes designed for AS and A2 students (see later in this section). Do not neglect the 'virtual' world however; online conferences, blogs, forums and social utility websites, when safely used, can also provide this opportunity to meet and communicate with new people.

♦ *Ensure an accessible wide range of up-to-date resources*: Many G&T students wish to work in the environment of their choice. This may be at home, in the school library or with friends at their house. What they want is the freedom to choose where they work and not be fixed to a set environment determined solely by resource availability. In the working world employers are moving towards flexible working to support the demands of modern family life. Schools and colleges are also moving towards more flexible learning through the development of VLEs as discussed in Chapter One and extended schools. Work can be checked online by the teacher rather than waiting for the hand in deadline, questions can be raised through online forums and resources retrieved through networked access rather than reading from the text book. In 2008 YGT launched a range of post 16 support materials for online learning at home. The materials are designed to complement examination course material and are designed to promote independent study and shared discussion. These materials represent recognition of the need and demand for post-16 extension material for G&T students.

For the more-able learner the importance lies in their ability to choose when and how they work and to explore avenues of personal interest, not be held prisoner by the exam specification. A post-16 G&T student is able to make the informed decision but they require the teacher or another adults' support in doing so. They are still learners and working outside of the classroom does not mean abandoning their learning needs; instead it means supporting their learning through different communication medium.

♦ *Mentoring*: There is a Chinese proverb which relates to the best way to learn is by teaching someone else. 'I hear and I forget. I see and I remember. I do and I understand.' A Latin proverb similarly cites, 'By learning you will teach; by teaching you will understand.' Many students claim to learn more effectively when they are asked to teach someone else. Talented young sportsmen and women have traditionally played a role in coaching their junior team mates and gradually this practice is being more readily used in an academic environment. G&T students are often now given the opportunity to act as mentors to other students and support their learning journey through school. Often this can take the form of supporting less-able students and helping them 'get better' at a targeted subject or skill. An alternative and arguably more challenging process is for post-16 G&T students to mentor younger G&T pupils. This can be more testing for the mentor as the mentee will often challenge the thinking of the mentor in contrast to a less-able mentee who is more inclined to accept the mentor's help or advice without challenge. A post-16 student will have to prepare for such session and consider how they will access the learning and support for their mentee. They will not want to be caught out intellectually by someone younger and supposedly less informed than they. An ideal opportunity for mentoring can be between AS and GCSE students. Subject knowledge will be relatively fresh and the transition process for the future AS student will be aided by individual relationships being established.

♦ *Extension and enrichment programmes*: Summer schools and master classes have grown in availability in the last ten years due to the work of NAGTY, YGT, Aimhigher and other supporting bodies. Single day activities and conference are growing in number often led by subject organizations, museums or study centres. Whilst many summer programmes such as Warwick University's IGGY Summer U is aimed at 11–16-year olds there are programmes specifically for 16–18-year olds. YGT promote available master classes and summer schools as should your local university or Open University provider. The G&T coordinator or Sixth Form or college leader should be e-mailed or sent the relevant literature and may need to be prompted to pass it on.

♦ *Links with universities*: If you are lucky enough to live in a university town and have access to the campus, the local university can be an extremely useful resource. Students can visit the university, attend lectures as well as access the resources; conversely the university can visit the students. Undergraduates may welcome the opportunity to work with AS and A2 G&T students in the same way the AS student may mentor the G&T GCSE pupil. Lecturers and graduates may be willing to share their work with a small group of interested and capable AS and A2 students. Some AS and A2 students will be the first in their family to receive further education and the notion of higher education can in some circumstances be alien and unsupported within the family environment. For a G&T student from this background – to be able to enter the world of a university undergraduate is an aspiration raising and potentially life-changing experience.

♦ *Agencies*: Many organizations are worth being aware of simply to flag up with students, their families and the school G&T coordinator. Aim Higher is a DCFS initiative working in partnership with the Higher Education Funding Council for England (HEFCE) with the remit to widen participation in UK higher education. A key student target area is communities where there is no tradition of young people going to university or college. This may be a consequence of, for example, economic, ethnic and medical factors and provision is made to overcome these difficulties through mentoring programmes, summer schools and other residential courses, online information and help for gaining financial support. In 2008 YGT launched a range of post-16 support materials for online learning at home. The materials are designed to complement examination course material and are designed to promote independent study and shared discussion. These materials represent recognition of the need and demand for post-16 extension material for gifted and talented students.

There is a world of opportunity available beyond the classroom for all students and especially for more-able learners designed to extend their thinking and understanding of their world and how they can change it through learning. Teachers can steer their most-able students in the right direction and show them opportunities that are available to them. At post-16 they will also need to take hold of the initiative themselves and through a simple measure such as a G&T notice board or message board they can be made aware of what their community and region can offer their learning.

Summary

Gifted and talented opportunities outside the classroom have grown significantly over the last few years and there are financial support structures available to support low-income families. Ask your G&T coordinator to keep you informed of subject-specific activities and take a regular look at the YGT website. Many post-16 activities require you as a sponsor but not as an attendee so do not feel that you have not got the time; the emphasis is on the student working independently not with their teacher.

23. G&T preparation for examinations

If you are willing to deal effectively with the needs of the most able pupils you will raise the achievement of all pupils.

Mike Tomlinson, former director of OfSTED

Preparation for examination at AS and A2 for all students is covered through ideas in Chapters Three and Five but there are some aspects of examinations which are more relevant to the needs of the more-able learner. The increasing range of pathways available to post-16 through the personalization agenda has resulted in a deviation from the traditional AS and A2 route for many students and an increase in the range and type of examinations many post-16 students are entered for. This section is not about the teaching and learning strategies for examinations but instead examination opportunities available to the most-able learners. Exam achievement does not equate to knowing and loving a subject or being a master of it but it is an essential aspect of our education and employment system and students should not be deprived an opportunity to meet their potential. Over-emphasis on this area will restrict a student's development in their chosen subject area. Below are ten suggestions for extending G&T AS and A2 students' examination potential, references to other chapters are made throughout.

◆ *Feedback*: Assessment for learning remains at the top of the personalization agenda and the G&T agenda. If students have clear targets and a sense of progression and how to get better at their subject they will improve. The key to feedback for more-able students is to aim straight for the top and do not force the students to jump through hoops to get there. To clarify this point consider the way music grading systems work – a student is entered for level six piano because their teacher recognizes their ability and believes they can cope with the standard of the examination. Prior learning allows the student to be at that standard. The grading teacher does not make the student prove they can achieve grades 1–5 during the examination, the student simply plays to the best of their ability and the student either passes or fails. If they pass they are encouraged to move onto the next grade and if they fail they are set clear targets for improvement in order that they can achieve the grade next time. The merits of this system are not for debate here the important point is that the ability of the student is taken for granted and they are being shown how to improve further with clear guidance and direction. To what extent do you feedback in this manner to your most-able students? Do they have to repeatedly jump through the hoops both teacher and student already know they can do or is the student constantly being encouraged to aim higher through the use of achievable yet challenging next step targets. Each student should have targets unique to their current stage of development and understand how to get better. It does not make the getting better any easier but the sense of satisfaction when it is achieved is immeasurable for both student and teacher.

◆ *Use of criteria and level descriptors*: Most students need to feel secure in their learning and move forward at a pace suitable to their development. A teacher may choose not to share the criteria for the highest grades with some students as it may damage self-esteem and make them feel inadequate. A more-able student is more likely to want to be made aware of what it takes to achieve a high grade and what they need to do to achieve it. Share the highest level criteria with your most-able students from the start. Challenge their learning with the grade descriptors and set them such goals as a problem to solve. Many able students will have coasted through their school life up to this point and AS will be the first examination which has made them think about how they express their understanding. Many G&T students begin to enjoy their learning at 16 and the sense of achievement for them is all the greater when they have really had to work to succeed. The exam and the grade criteria is not a secret and students should be encouraged to interpret it and make it their own.

◆ *Specifications*: Share the specifications and extend more-able students knowledge base by encouraging independent reading and exploration of the specification using techniques discussed in Chapter Two.

◆ *Reading lists*: Not all G&T students love to read and for some it will rapidly switch them off from their passion for the subject.

Deviate from the regular list and look for reading material that will suit the individual student. Magazines, journals, biography, autobiography, travel writing, manuals, websites, forums and blogs all require reading and can bring a subject to life in a manner beyond the classroom text.

♦ *Extension papers*: New examination specifications have been introduced for teaching at AS in 2008 and A2 in 2009, the A* grade is a real possibility.

♦ *Model*: Modelling of work to demonstrate to a student what the teacher wants a student to achieve is a commonly used approach to learning and can work effectively with most learners. One concern with modelling work for G&T students is that it can make the intended outcome formulaic and dull thus restricting the individual student's creativity and willingness to experiment. This is a cautionary word to use modelling with the most-able reservedly and only if they genuinely cannot find a way through the task independently. Alternatively model work from the next stage of learning to provide an aspirational model. An undergraduate piece of work may provide a challenge to the student and motivate them to reach such heights of success.

♦ *Seek external advice*: Not every Olympic Gold Medallist or Nobel Prize Winner has been taught by an Olympic Gold Medallist or Nobel Prize Winner. Teachers will at certain points in their career meet and teach students far more gifted and talented in the subject than they are. On these occasions experience and inspiration become a teacher's greatest possession and coaching the potential from the student and motivating them to achieve more become the role of the teacher. At times a teacher may need to seek advice on how to best serve the interest of an individual student and this is to be commended, not seen as a sign of weakness. Academics and experts in the field are becoming increasingly willing to work with post-16 students and welcome opportunities to do so enhancing the learning of the student and the teacher.

♦ *International Baccalaureate*: In September 2008 AQA introduced the International Baccalaureate. The examination is designed to work as a compliment to a student's other AS courses or as a stand alone alternative to traditional AS and A2 papers. The extended project or individual study project or thesis is designed to demonstrate writing skill and the ability to develop an argument. It can be completed as part of an AS exam and allows students to produce an outcome which extends their interest in an area, skill or intellectual ability. This ideally lends itself to a G&T student by encouraging them to move onto a higher plane of thinking. Further papers are available in critical thinking, citizenship or general studies; it will also highlight community work they have been involved in. The International Baccalaureate has the potential to engage and captivate its learners and enhance subject teaching and the breadth of opportunity subject classrooms can offer. It can free teachers from the confines of a single specification and allow teachers to educate students to be masters of their subject domain and not solely prepare them for an examination in their subject.

24. G&T celebrations

To complete this chapter it is important to remember that all students deserve recognition for their achievements however large or small. It is a complaint of younger G&T pupils that they often feel overlooked in terms of school rewards. Pupils who make progress or significant leaps in their learning can be acknowledged but a consistently high achiever can often be overlooked within the school reward system.

At AS and A2 success is often celebrated through examination results which usually appear outside of term time and once students have left their teacher. Most learners enjoy acknowledgment for their industry however old or young and post-16 students deserve recognition for their endeavours and achievements on a regular basis. At post-16 this may need to take a different form from mainstream reward systems and needs to be meaningful to the student concerned.

Celebration events can add a whole college or Sixth Form dimension to the honour of an individual's learning and provide an external audience to everyday learning. Invite parents, governors, local organizations and the press to share the experiences, achievements and outcomes generating from young people's every day learning opportunities. This can also create a positive home-school link which can often be lost in post-16 institutions of learning. More-able students will benefit from the acknowledgement such events provide especially when the processes of their work are as celebrated as the end product itself.

G&T students can seek recognition for their work away for the classroom in the shape of competitions and events. Subject associations and media organizations often run events and competitions which would hold appeal to a more-able student and add an extra dimension of challenge to their learning. An event or challenge can provide the audience the teacher may be looking for to add a realism and sense of purpose to work being undertaken through the exam course.

Chapter summary

Gifted and talented education is about inclusion not exclusion. It is designed to draw more-able learners into the learning process and remove any imposed ceiling to their learning. Many opportunities and activities discussed in this chapter are not exclusive to G&T students; they will work with many students but they provide the extended thinking and learning experiences that more-able students crave. Consider the group you teach and whether the opportunities to help them extend their own boundaries are in place and how the curriculum can be opened up for them. Explore some of the suggested strategies within your own subject and seek the advice of the leading teacher or coordinator if you need clarification on an idea.

5 | Revision

In the current educational system, the educational success of a post-16 student is measured by their examination results. These results in turn allow teachers, school leaders, students, parents and other stakeholders to measure the exam performance of a school or college both in terms of the statistical pass rates of the institution or increasingly through value added performance statistics. Value added measures have been used in the DCSF Achievement and Attainment Tables since 2002. They measure the attainment of students in comparison to students with similar prior attainment; this is deemed fairer than using raw outcomes. In 2006 a new model of value added measures known as Contextual Value Added (CVA) was introduced, aiming to take account of the many other factors that relate to student progress and achievement. The DCSF Post-16 CVA model of 2006 includes the following attainment and contextual factors:

◆ Student prior attainment;
◆ Student volume of level 3 qualifications;
◆ Student qualification route;
◆ Student gender;
◆ Cohort average and range of prior attainment;
◆ Cohort size;
◆ Interaction terms between the previous factors.

The post-16 CVA is measured at the end of Key stage 5 and includes all level 3 qualifications. Through a calculation of factors by their respective coefficients a student is given a prediction of their total level 3 points score. Each student's actual outcome is compared with the prediction provided by the model; if their outcome is higher than the predicted total, their progress is above expectation and their contribution to their school or colleges CVA will be positive. A score below prediction will result in a negative CVA score. Finally all individual student scores are summed and averaged for each college or school.

It is the role of college leaders to look at the performance trends of their educational establishment and development plan accordingly for the future. Sixth Form leaders are under immense pressure from their counter-parts at the Local Authority and the DCSF as well as OfSTED and HMI to meet performance targets. The analysis of performance indicators occupies vast quantities of school resources and when used in an informed manner can provide teachers with insightful and useful student data and information. (For further discussion of the effective use of summative and formative data refer to Chapter Three).

Examination performance published through Achievement and Attainment Tables is central to the perceived reputation of a college or Sixth Form centre within its local community. Examination results above the local or national average can result in a strong student population, with dedicated parental support. The financial implications of losing this support are immense and can result in the loss of subject opportunities and ultimately jobs. In turn this reinforces the general understanding that examination results place schools and colleges under a great deal of pressure. They matter, not only, to the student whose future life will be directly affected by them but on the overall standards within a college or school. As teachers, it is our ultimate responsibility to ensure that we do everything within our control to enable our students to perform at or beyond their identified potential.

25. The paradox of examination

Discussion of examination results, corresponding attainment tables and CVA leads to an apparent paradox: how can teachers create independent learners and a captivating classroom when they have to ensure that they are teaching in a way that ensures students achieve the best possible exam results? Is this not the reality of post-16 education? Teachers want to create a more engaging classroom but work in an environment where they are pressured to achieve results; teachers will ultimately resort to 'spoon-feeding' students and drilling them for the examination; training them to pass and not to think.

When I found myself following a path of training students for their examination and not teaching them to be historians, I began to research and formulate much of the thinking already explored in this book. I reminded myself to separate my pedagogic thinking between educating students and preparing them for the exam. The exam specification drives the content of my lessons in the same way the assessment objectives as laid out on the syllabus, structure the lesson progression. Yet the lessons are far removed from spoon-feeding and exam instruction. I aim to make effective use of a range of teaching and learning strategies nevertheless throughout the course I try to maintain an awareness of the students need to feel secure and prepared for their examination. Fundamental to achieving this is the key role of revision.

By means of planned, structured and pleasurable revision strategies students can be fully prepared for the momentous examination while at the same time retaining their independence and motivation. Therefore while effective teaching and learning remains the driving force to develop students' subject passion and motivation to learn, there is a real need to prepare and equip students for the examination they will sit. This chapter considers the role revision has to play in preparing students for an exam and how teachers can provide students with the necessary tools to be able to revise and prepare for the most important days of their educational life thus far.

Students are sometimes taught how to revise but student interviews (see Chapter Four) indicate that students are less frequently taught the formal skills of revision. Whose responsibility is it to do this? A subject teacher is concerned with their subject and the delivery of the syllabus and beyond, as well as developing subject specific concepts and knowledge. A tutor may be looking out for the social and emotional and future needs of their tutee and not be able to spend time with more generic learning skills. The key skills programme as discussed in Chapter One, aims to develop students' transitional skills as well as their skills of communication, synthesis and presentation. Therefore do teachers make assumptions that because the students have made it to 'A' Level and achieved C grades and above in most of their GCSEs or level 2 equivalents that they are able to revise and remember vast quantities of information with relatively little guidance? A G&T Year 11 student at a Norfolk high school commented that by the end of their high school career they 'knew lots but had no idea how to learn or apply it'.

A subject teacher has to take a degree of responsibility for their students being fully prepared for their examination but simply revisiting and repeating information already learned is not sufficient to teach a student to revise and learn independently. To use revision techniques in an explicit manner with students when revising subject content offers a far more helpful balance of knowledge and learning, which the student can subsequently employ independently. With encouragement and shared practice amongst teachers, the student may be able to seize the techniques drawn on and utilize them outside of the subject they have been delivered in. All students have a preference for different learning styles and there is no 'best fit' method of revision; it would therefore be helpful to use a range of revision techniques with students to allow them to choose their own route through revision with a full armoury of strategies to use at the appropriate moment in their exam preparation.

When using a particular strategy in the classroom the student will benefit from an opportunity to reflect upon the technique used and tease out with their teacher an understanding of which aspects of the particular method did or did not work for them. This meta-cognitive approach to revision will be helpful for the transferability of the strategy used and help them to identify further, not only which particular method would work best but why the chosen process specifically enhanced revision of a given topic. Examples of the type of questions that could be given as student prompts are provided with the suggested revision strategies below.

Summary

Revision skills require teaching. Students have earned a place on an AS and A2 course because they are able and or hard working. The move to 'A' Level will require application of a much wider knowledge base than they are used to within a restricted time scale and immediate recall is an essential denominator of examination success. Revision is a whole class as well as independent activity and in both contexts it will benefit from a planned and structured approach. Furthermore students will profit from the opportunity to analyse the merits and demerits of chosen techniques in order that they can reuse and reapply preferred strategies.

26. Organization for learning

Preparing students for revision is challenging for most teachers because it can be an area of learning that falls outside perceived classroom responsibility. If teachers aim to encourage independence then over-structuring and helping prepare student revision could arguably be counter-productive and result in a reversion to a 'spoon-fed' approach to learning. There are methods of effective classroom practice and smart use of homework that enable students to be organized and equipped for revision. These suggestions are designed to encourage both an academically disciplined classroom and to provide students with an ability to organize their work that will pay dividends later on, especially during examination revision. Many of these foundations of learning should not be left until the students are 16, in fact they will be more beneficial if used from an earlier age and are part of a students tool-box of learning.

Classwork. This is the basis of all their future work, including revision, so be thorough from the start. Tell students to:

♦ use a folder;
♦ invest in dividers;
♦ organize your notes into sections;
♦ use the exam specification as a guide and have one section syllabus section;
♦ clear contents page and any subject specific references or formulas at the front;
♦ place your notes and classwork in behind;
♦ comment and target sheet at the front of the folder for feedback and next steps targets (see Chapter Three).

Homework. This needs to be organized on the same basis and complement students' classwork. It needs to be purposeful and meaningful to the topic of study and the work within the classroom. Homework is an opportunity to build trust with students and encourage their independence and this is explored further in Chapter Two. Homework is not always a visible outcome and although it need not always be marked or assessed, it must be acknowledged otherwise students will begin to devalue and lose their motivation to complete it. Place value on homework by checking it has been done and acknowledging it immediately, at least verbally or through a classroom activity that is dependent on homework having been completed. Encourage students to take the following steps for homework in order that revision will be straightforward when the time comes.

◆ Log it.
◆ The task has been given for a purpose – DO IT!
◆ Keep it legible for future reference.
◆ Back it up or create a hard copy.
◆ File it in the correct place.
◆ Check it.
◆ Use it.

Targets from feedback. This is discussed in depth in Chapter Three but is important in setting the tone of classwork and the discipline of a classroom referred to earlier. It is necessary for students to respond to their feedback immediately in order that the corrected work is there for revision and not the un-amended work or worst of all incorrect work. Promptly responding to targets allows the students to reprocess their work, this by definition is 'revision' and will aid memory based revision later on. Encouraging students to organize; review and process their work and make use of the advice they have been given in their feedback is a skill they can easily transfer from subject to subject. It will also save reworking of notes at the end of the course and during exam preparation time.

Electronic work. Many students word process their work and keep files on their home computers and Sixth Form profiles rather than print the end product. Whilst commendable for reducing our carbon-footprint, this paper free approach can cause problems when it comes to checking work and particularly for revision as a teacher will not have hard copies of work to comment on and assess. Systems can be employed to help with electronic files and are to be actively encouraged by the Sixth Form centre and colleges themselves. Keep back up copies of all work on a memory stick, ideally one per subject to aid organization.

◆ Make use of a school e-mail to encourage students to e-mail their work to the teacher for comments and feedback, this provides another form of back up.
◆ Print revised and amended work which has been amended and improved through use of feedback comments, hard copies are important to maintain a subject progress file of classwork and independent work.

As discussed in earlier chapters many students will enjoy engaging with online learning as for many this is a preferred form of communication. Their frequent use of social utility sites and virtual communication makes this an efficient use of their time.

◆ Make use of a school VLE to encourage dialogue between teacher and student, and student and student, this will reinforce understanding and encourage a virtual conversation thus acting as a method of revision.
◆ Set a forum for revision topics and change the revision topic every two to three days and set the expectation that students will contribute.

Planning. Planning revision is essential. January or May can seem a long way off for students but if they are encouraged to look at the demands of the whole exam timetable as well as regular school work and their part time job as well as leisure activities there are very few hours left in a day, week or term. Joint plan a timetable with your students so they can determine which areas of the course they wish to develop with teacher's help and which areas they wish to pursue independently. Provide the students with hard copy or electronic timetables and as far as possible keep to the agreed agenda to model and reinforce the importance of forward planning and keeping to a schedule. This joint approach to planning is helpful to you and the student as it maps the medium-term sequence of lessons and shares the ownership and responsibility for learning.

Materials

What do students actually need to be able to revise effectively? Schools and colleges are not usually in a financially advantageous position to grant each student text books, revision guides and extra reading. Ethically we cannot expect students to be able to purchase their own revision guides and materials and it is wise to consider the value for money such products offer. The VLE offers an amazing online revision opportunity but accessibility needs to be considered. Ultimately a set of well-organized and thorough notes and assessments should be all that the student requires but as discussed in Chapter One the long-term value of notes is questionable and many students do not take notes with a view to using them for later revision. If techniques for making notes are delivered using strategies outlined in Chapter One this difficulty may be overcome but the issue of what do they revise from must be addressed. Below is a list of suggested materials to share with students for revision purposes, with discussion of their respective strengths and limitations.

Strengths

◆ *Notes*: Use the techniques discussed in Chapter One to create a set of durable notes which can be used for long-term revision rather than immediate planning.

◆ *Classwork*: The main tool for revision and most effective when the work has been regularly fed back on.

◆ *VLE*: Post a range of materials to extend student knowledge and evaluation and encourage students to share their research, articles, weblinks with their peers.

◆ *Websites*: A fantastic research tool but can be of less use for revision, there are some specifically designed for revision and these are helpful for testing knowledge but provide little extension thinking, it is helpful for the class to create its own recommended list of websites that aid revision and help to reinforce and consolidate learning rather than extend it through a recommended list.

◆ *Revision guides*: More of a security blanket than an aid to learning, revision guides are a mass market and many college departments financially support the purchase of them. They are up-to-date and directly linked to the exam course and offer helpful tips from examination officers and markers. They are particularly useful for sample answers and if combined with 'Assessment for Learning Techniques' from Chapter Three can be of immense benefit to students.

Limitations

◆ *Notes*: Notes taken early in the course will be less effective than those taken later and students will need to be alerted to the limitation and probable weaknesses in this early work.

◆ *Classwork*: Unless techniques previously discussed are employed students will devalue their classwork and turn to other quick fix solutions; this is their own revision manual and must be respected as such from the start of the course.

◆ *VLE*: This requires teacher monitoring and intervention and will need to be accessible to all to ensure equity and accuracy.

◆ *Websites*: Students can waste many valuable hours trawling and discovering new information when the emphasis should be on reinforcement and consolidation of knowledge; encourage the use of selected, recommended sites.
◆ *Revision guides*: These are designed as training manuals and will show students tricks of the trade through tips from the examiners and those in the know; they can remove individuality and make a student lazy in the use of their own work and research.

Summary

Students can view their classwork and homework as distinct from revision materials. By equipping students with the organizational tools necessary for advanced learning from the outset of their course they can make greater use of classwork and homework when revision looms. Over dependency on new materials when revision begins can devalue students' prior learning and homogenize their learning into a stream of bite-size gobbets of information. Revision can be identified as an integral part of learning from the beginning of AS and A2 with regular reinforcement of learning strategies throughout the course. Supporting students' organization of learning will pay dividends in subsequent revision and ultimately their results.

27. Environment for learning

Many educational institutions are currently undergoing building programmes and cosmetic make overs in the quest to design an ideal learning environment. Funding from the private sector through the Private Funding Initiative (PFI) programme has enabled architects and school leaders to design ergonomic learning environments to enhance the scholarly atmosphere for students and staff alike. In Sixth Form colleges this has meant expanded libraries, improved ICT facilities and recreational areas for relaxation and socialization. In a recent conversation with a director of a Sixth Form college that had undergone such a transformation I asked if he felt the environment had improved learning, he replied, 'The environment helps but it is the guidance the students receive that leads their learning.' I considered this in relation to revision and whether the environment or the guidance is paramount to the student. Consider, for example, a student called Sam who is the eldest of four children in the family; Mum works nights and Dad works irregular hours; as the eldest child, Sam is expected to care for the other children in the family and help with domestic chores; Sam shares a room with a younger sibling who enjoys noisy electronic pursuits in the shared bedroom. Where is Sam; supposed to study? How will Sam's home environment impact on his ability to study or revise? Which is of greater importance to Sam environment or guidance?

Sam will rely on his college environment for a calm atmosphere in which to complete his studies and his revision. He will find home study difficult and all the guidance the teacher offers him will be meaningless if there is nowhere to independently put it into practice. Sam's situation is not particularly unusual and it is essential as teachers to be aware of the challenges many of our students face in understanding or achieving a suitable study environment. The following advice may be helpful to share with your students and make sure consideration is given to those who may need to find alternatives.

Revise independently

Your Space. Appreciate with the students that not everyone is lucky enough to have their own bedroom or study. Reassure them that this does not matter and what is important is that a student tries to create his/her own space for revision. Communicate with families through parents and open evenings the idea of a student using a room at a set time when they will not be disturbed. If this is not possible investigate the use a local library or quiet corner of a café. Reinforce the importance for students to feel calm and focused when revising and that the environment helps create that.

Free from Interruption. Experiment in class with interruption free learning and see how challenging students find it to keep on task. Conversely keep interrupting their study with messages, phone calls, a piece of gossip or switching the DVD player on to reinforce how hugely disruptive such interferences can be. Discuss the need for interruption free learning and how this can easily be achieved by turning off mobile phones, taking the computer off line, and ignoring the land line phone. Their reward can be turning the phone back on and telling someone how pleased they are with what they have achieved.

Access to Snacks and Drinks. Evidence has shown that our brains work better if they are hydrated; so advise students to drink lots of water and keep their sugar levels up with fruit and healthy snacks. Encourage them to pause for a two minute break every twenty minutes to refuel or relax their mind.

Rewards. Remember the mobile phone reward mentioned earlier. Make rewards charts in class for completing revision tasks and keeping to the plan. Is this too childish or patronizing? Absolutely, but if it helps this is not a problem? Remember to stress the big rewards come after the exams and on results day.

Revision in college

To an extent the college or Sixth Form environment is largely out of a single teacher's control as is the students' use of their study periods. However as a teacher you can set the tone of learning in your regular environment and you can try to teach lessons outside of the classroom to show your students the value of different learning environments. If a teacher were to introduce a new skill, activity or style or working the teacher may employ a modelling technique to demonstrate the method to the students. Similarly how to work in different environments can also be modelled for students. Instead of telling students to go to the library to research or complete a task take them there yourself and conduct the lesson in the library or study centre. This will have two advantages; it will show them the etiquette of working in a different location by introducing them to the surroundings in a constructive fashion; second, it will be refreshing for students to work outside of the confines of the usual classroom setting. If you are lucky enough to be near a public library, college or even university organize a short visit there with your students to show them a different place of learning and how the atmosphere can be conducive to intense and focused study away from the usual comforts and distractions.

Summary

Post-16 students no longer learn in a traditional setting at designated times. Irregular hours and use of mobile technology enable students to study at times and in places that are suitable for them. There is scope however for introducing them to different learning environments and highlighting the benefits of uninterrupted time. Model different learning environments in class in order that students can make an informed decision about when and where they wish to study. This in turn increases the level of individual responsibility towards their learning and increases their independence as learners.

28. Techniques for revising independently

Techniques for revision have been researched, documented and often discredited and redesigned based on new educational research. How students learn occupies vast annals of academic research. This book is not designed to test educational research and differing theories of how students most effectively revise. Instead it is designed to offer a range of techniques and encourage teachers to experiment with them within the context of their own classrooms with their own students. It is important for the students that they are exposed to a range of techniques in order that they can decide the ones that suit their approach to learning. Visual learning works well for many 'A' Level students but not for all and the way we prefer to learn will not suit all our students. Try to offer students the opportunity to experiment and practice with the different strategies by planning for opportunities to build them into them into your lessons. In order to help the students make informed decisions about which methods work most effectively with different types of information and outcomes a full debrief of the mode of learning that has taken place is fundamental to the students' future application of the given technique.

Use different techniques within the same lesson to offer a comparison of learning styles or apply a single revision method for a specified assessment objective or topic and consider its application in different circumstances. This still allows the teacher to deliver content as well as adding a meta-cognitive dimension to the lesson which is of long-term benefit to the students.

There now follows a series of revision strategies, each with an example of how they can be used in different subject areas, where they can be used within a lesson and finally questions for a teacher to pose to students following use of the revision technique to promote consideration of the strengths and weaknesses of that particular method or approach to revision.

Forums and Blogs

This is designed to encourage interaction with and reflection of a given topic of study. Using the VLE or an alternative online forum students enter into dialogue about the revision they have undertaken and the knowledge they have acquired with their classmates online. They can discuss the style of revision they used or the new learning that has taken place. Either way the student is engaging with the topic of study and interacting with other students to enhance their knowledge, understanding and application of their subject.

1. Post a question to the students on the VLE or an online forum from a past paper or examination board sample assessment material (SAMs).
2. Set a time limit for the discussion and use the talk rules from Chapter One to ensure extended not repetitive debate.
3. When the discussion has closed set the same question in class to ensure immediate follow up.
4. Post feedback from the written responses on the VLE or online forum and invite students to respond to the feedback or extend their ideas further.
5. Close the debate shortly afterward and quickly move on to another topic.

Other ideas for using forums and blogs for revision:

◆ Divide up revision strategies between students in your class and ask the students to keep a blog of their experience and level of success they are finding with their strategies.
◆ Encourage students to investigate other methods of revision and post them on the forum or blog for others to make use of.
◆ Link up with another college or Sixth Form to give a broader experience of the topic and approaches to revision.
◆ Questions to ask:

◇ How did the realization that your knowledge and understanding was in a public domain affect the way you posted your online comment?

◇ Which comments on the forum extended your thinking or forced you to return to your research?

◇ How did the online dialogue differ from face to face discussion?

◇ What are the weaknesses of using this approach to learning and how does it compare to other techniques?

Record/Talk

If a song plays on the radio many people are often able to sing along having heard it only a few times.

1. If voice recorders are available use audio equipment to create a podcast of a topic, conceptual analysis, suggested question response or practical experiment/field study.
2. Listen to it at the start or end of a lesson.
3. Students are to write down all they can remember from the recording.
4. Ask a question relating to the content of the clip and ask students to discuss their response in pairs with or without notes.

It can also be used in the following ways:

◆ Stop the recording at regular intervals and ask students to write down what happens next.

◆ Turn the volume down on key words and phrases and ask students what the missing words might be.

◆ Encourage students to create their own audio notes using their condensed notes and play them on the bus on the way to college.

◆ If the college intranet allows store the podcasts for open access by other students.

◆ Compile recordings onto a CD and copy for use by all students.

◆ Questions to ask:

◇ Deconstruct the recording and ask what is it about the recording that helps the listener remember the content of the recording.

◇ How could this be improved further?

◇ What makes an effective podcast?

◇ What attributes does an effective speaker and listener need to have?

Movie files

This is a variation on the record/talk technique but this time with visuals as well as commentary. This can be time consuming and the students can become pre-occupied with the creativity of the task rather than the content and revision purpose behind it.

1. Pose a question to the students from a past paper or SAMs
2. Using movie maker or storyboarding software and ask students to create a 60 second movie file to answer the question set.
3. Show the film over a series of lessons for reinforcement.
4. Save the film for revision or use the previous year's group work in a revision lesson.
5. Use any of the previous strategies to test knowledge.

Other ideas for using movies for revision:

◆ Write a review of the movie focusing on the content.
◆ Answer an examination question using knowledge from the movie.
◆ Write a narrative to accompany the movie and address any gaps in content.
◆ Compile movies onto a DVD and copy for use by all students.
◆ Questions to ask:

◇ Deconstruct the movie and ask what is it about the choice of images that helps the viewer remember the content of the recording.
◇ Look at films of other groups and ask is this an effective film to help me remember.
◇ What are the weaknesses of using this approach to learning and how does it compare to other techniques?

Memory maps

Memory maps are best used when linking topics and creating themes or ideas. This can be done with or without notes but should be done without as the exam gets closer. A good tip to give your students is to use a pencil so they can rub information out and always write on the line.

1. Pose an examination question from a past paper or SAMs
2. Place the key question in the centre of a page of A3
3. Using the relevant notes and resources create branches on the mind map.
4. The next layer of branches should be key points to support these points.
5. As the student moves outwards on their memory map they should become more specific with evidence.
6. Advise the student to look for links and join up connecting areas.

It can also be used in the following ways:

◆ Rotate the memory maps around the classroom and ask students to add to each other's work; pencils are very helpful for this.
◆ For a quicker activity ask students to work on one branch only and then create a whole class map.
◆ Place a memory map at the front of each unit of work as a summary of the work ahead and as an 'at a glance' guide to the topic.
◆ Add symbols and images to the memory map to act as memory triggers.
◆ Questions to ask:

   ◇ What are the benefits of this approach to revising compared to using the condensed notes approach?
   ◇ Why is it helpful to write on the lines not at the ends like a traditional spider diagram?
   ◇ Where can the memory map be displayed to help further revision?

Re-writing

This is a good starting point for revision and allows students to refresh their understanding of topics that may have been studied many months ago.

1. Students re-read their existing notes on a chosen topic, concept, experiment using a skim reading technique.

2. Re-write 5 points from the notes just read.
3. Check the new notes against the original notes and list any gaps.
4. Repeat until all key points are learned and there are no gaps.

This is not an exciting approach yet it works for many students. If used early in the course the activity can reinforce the importance of effective note taking skills and increase the value of their preparatory work.

It can be used in the following ways:

◆ At the start of a lesson as a means of stressing the importance preparation work and note taking itself.
◆ After students have completed their first set of notes to evaluate the effectiveness of the notes and discuss further strategies for note taking afterwards.
◆ Repeat at 10 minute intervals rather than complete all stages in one go.
◆ As a plenary to evaluate the success of a note taking exercise.
◆ Allow a maximum of 10 minutes for the activity.
◆ Questions to ask:

◇ How important was the quality of the original notes to this exercise?
◇ How many re-writings did it take to learn the required content?
◇ What changes need to be made to the original notes to make them easier to learn from?

Condense

This technique shows a student how to cut their notes down into manageable and memorizable chunks.

1. Students look at their notes on a topic, concept or experiment;
2. Create four headings with no more than four words per heading;
3. Using their notes condense the original notes into one sentence for each heading;
4. Now condense into four keywords;
5. Students learn the keywords;
6. Students now rewrite in full prose about each of the keywords in the context of the syllabus or examination question.

It can also be used in the following ways:

◆ To check the effectiveness of each other's notes using peer-assessment strategies (see Chapter Three);
◆ As a game to see who has the most effective words;
◆ Put the final words on sticky notes and ask the students to talk for one minute on the topic using the chosen word only.
◆ Start the next lesson using the final words only and ask the students to discuss the topics with each other using the words only.
◆ Questions to ask:

◇ What attributes does an effective keyword need to have?
◇ What other strategies can be used to help remember the keywords?
◇ Which other subject areas could this strategy be used in?
◇ What changes need to be made to the original notes to make them easier to learn from?

Test

This is essential to make sure students are retaining knowledge.

◆ Ask students to prepare their own quizzes for revision lessons, the more interactive the better.
◆ Make use of hand-held decision making technology and the interactive whiteboard wherever possible.
◆ Use frequently and quickly and not just at then end of the course to ensure maximum opportunities for revisiting content in order that topics from September are not left until the summer for revision.

29. Revising in class and in groups

Each academic year, I meet my new AS or A2 group with high hopes and expectations. There is great excitement in the anticipation of the enthusiasm a new group of students will bring to the course and the satisfaction they will hopefully derive from their studies. When they are an enthusiastic group it can be tempting to extend their subject learning and not leave adequate lesson time for in-class revision lessons. One particular year I began to panic as the date of the exam rapidly approached blaming the situation on lost lessons caused by bank holidays; whereas other years I have berated the exam board for not providing enough notice of the examination timetable. Both are poor excuses for a fundamental weakness in my occasional failure to plan sufficient group revision time into my teaching schedule. Most years the problem never actually arises and somehow we finish the syllabus with a few weeks to spare to undertake whole class revision activities. Usually I summon my class to attend whole afternoons or mornings of revision during their study leave, they dutifully attend and usually leave more confident about the impending examination than when they arrived. Over many years I have experimented with a variety of revision strategies and as with all learning techniques the nature of the group is a determining factor in the success of each of the approaches to whole class revision. Below are my ten favourite techniques for whole class revision. The majority of students respond to the techniques with great enthusiasm due in part to the common feature of competition apparent in many of the strategies coupled with working against the clock (and prizes). It is worth noting that you will know your group inside out when it is time for revision and you can pitch tasks perfectly to the ability range of the group or individuals within the group.

Top ten in class activities for AS and 'A' Level revision

1. *Photographs*: This is a ridiculously easy revision technique that I discovered by default with my most recent AS class. Whilst involved in a prior lesson earlier in the year, I had photographed my class for use in their write up activity and for a class display. When planning the revision lesson for the same topic I was reminded of the photographs and decided to use them at the start of the lesson as an 'aide memoir'. The group watched the slide show run through a couple of times and after the initial merriment of ridiculing each other's appearances they watched the images with greater sobriety and began discussing the task and subject matter depicted in the images. A question and answer session of the topic of study evolved from the slide show and pushed their memory and thinking in a more gruelling way than I would otherwise have attempted. The visual stimulus and the enjoyment of the activity they had previously undertaken triggered a knowledge base that they had buried beyond their immediate recall. Arguably this method can only be successful if the

original activity was worthy of remembering. It can also be adapted to suit other visual stimuli.

2. *Sticky notes*: A favourite revision technique for many teachers is to ask students to condense information down into manageable and memorizable portions. Using sticky notes can again add diversity to an otherwise stale activity. Allow the students time to re-read or discuss the topic for revision using one of the other suggested strategies. Hand each student a sticky note and ask them to condense their knowledge into words that will fit on one side of the sticky note. Once they have completed this they will not be allowed to refer to their detailed notes for the remainder of the lesson or related activity. They must now use the sticky note in a follow up task such as an examination question or discussion. It is essential the notes on the sticky note are immediately applied to a task in order that the student can evaluate the usefulness of the knowledge they selected. As with all tasks, a full debrief is essential. This can be extended by exchanging notes and determining if they are able to use a classmate's work. In most instances they will not be able to and this is a useful insight into the importance of making their own revision notes rather than relying on manufactured or downloadable guides.

3. *Speed dating*: The purpose of speed dating is to impress the other person and hopefully meet someone you wish to have a relationship with. Speed dating for revision is similar in so far as the students are trying to impress someone they already know with their subject knowledge and the relationship they form will be with the subject matter. The students are given time to prepare notes they may keep with them at the date. They begin by sitting opposite a classmate and are given a fixed time period to impress their partner with their knowledge who is at liberty to ask questions of their speed dater. On the time signal, the students reverse questioning or move on to another 'date'. The value of this exercise as a revision tool is the repetitive nature of sharing the information as well as being challenged through informed questioning. Speed puts the students under pressure and the dating ensures the students are out to impress. Before the task begins provide students with a dating card to make comments about their potential date. At the end of the dating when everyone has spoken to everyone else ask students to mark their dating cards with who they would wish to date based on their knowledge and understanding of given questions.

4. *Examiners grade review meeting*: Students are usually surprised when informed of the process of examination marking, checking, moderating and grade review that takes place once their examinations are complete. The pressure on exam boards to mark, moderate and grade papers by the published deadlines is immense and examiners take care and pride in establishing the correct mark allocation, and grade boundaries. As a revision activity turn your classroom into an examiners meeting using students (past or present) practice examination questions. Insist on a formality to the meeting, photocopy papers in advance and provide name badges or labels. Organize the room into a conference room or café style layout and arrange to have pencils, water and sweets at each table to give the room a different atmosphere. The teacher plays the role of the Chief Examiner and appoints a Team Leader to each table who in turn instructs their examiners on what to do. The meeting could be for the purpose of marking and moderating examination papers using agreed criteria and mark schemes or it could be using marked papers to determine grade boundaries. Try to throw a few poorly marked examinations into the selection to keep markers on their toes and keep a formal atmosphere throughout the session. Ask the students to write an examiners report using a recent one as a model, on their findings with comments on areas of strength and targets for improvement. This can subsequently be used by teachers and students.

5. *Lesson starters and plenaries:* By this stage in their AS or A2 course students should be familiar with the use of starters and plenaries and may have already experimented with presenting a few themselves using the suggestions from Chapter Three. Revision is not the appropriate place for students to be delivering their own presentations as they should be processing previously acquired knowledge rather than engaging with new learning. It can however be helpful for a student to start the lesson with a prepared starter activity which involves all the class and encourages class revision from the moment the students enter the lesson. Through the preparation process the student will be revising and by preparing a starter activity the student will engage in a consideration of revision methods and techniques as well as how to help others learn. Set a time limit for the activity as students, like trainee teachers, have a tendency to misjudge how long a task can take to execute and be prepared as the teacher, to intervene if the other

students are not learning from the planned activity or it is simply taking too long. A similar activity and equally effective is to ask a student to conduct the plenary at the end of a topic or lesson. This does not need to be prepared for in advance and a forewarned student will remain attentive throughout the lesson if they know it is their role to summarize the learning from the lesson. By filming the starters and plenaries the teacher has a ready made resource to upload into the VLE.

6. *Past papers*: A tried and tested technique and frequently used by many teachers but worthy of note and when used with reflective learning strategies from Chapter Three, it is a very powerful tool. Past papers can be dull and repetitive however and rapid and regular use of past examination papers is much more effective than whole lessons of past papers. Employ an element of competition or surprise to the lesson, to liven up the use of past papers, through techniques such as past paper lottery. This involves students selecting the year of the past paper from a bag or bingo machine. Play a version of the classic game show 'Jeopardy' where students have to guess the question on the exam paper based on what would be in the answer or time students to give as many correct responses to a question in a given time frame.

7. *Previous students work*: Many of the reflective learner techniques discussed in Chapter Three work effectively during revision and examination practice. Studying student responses to exam questions provides students with a framework and structure to guide them when are first preparing for the examination. Using sample answers can help to make sense of a mark scheme especially if students are able to visualize what a Grade C or Grade A response looks like. Students can make more effective use of criteria and examination mark schemes at the end of the course and are in a better position to take their knowledge and understanding from across the syllabus into account rather than a snapshot view, as would be the case earlier on. Many students are confident to have their examination practice peer assessed and are able to use the feedback constructively. This can be daunting at the start of a revision and examination programme however and it can be more effective to make use of a previous students work for this purpose. Students will rarely hold back their critique if they are aware that the author is unknown to them. To facilitate this, create a portfolio of student work from all grade boundaries to share with future classes. If this is your first time through a course

consult with colleagues for examples or write a range of model answers yourself to share with the students, remembering not to make them too good.

8. *Rewrite the revision guide*: As previously discussed open market and downloadable revision guides have their role in a student's revision tool kit. A useful group activity is to create a class revision guide with everyone contributing and printing and distributing the end product or publishing it on the VLE. To promote common ownership share out the responsibility of content and agree a standardized format and layout which everyone has to stick to. Appointing an editor can be helpful but is by no means essential. If planned well in advance students can utilize their file notes for their area of the guide and revise them when necessary for the final publication.

9. *Memory maps*: These have been discussed in detail in Chapter One and Four and play a very important role in revision. For whole class revision activities the emphasis moves form the individual to small groups and students share and debated their ideas rather than make individual decisions. The process of small group talk and requests for explanation and further information encourage clarity and certainty. By selecting the right answer with peers and explaining and justifying choices to someone, information and analysis is more readily fixed in the mind. For revision purposes it helps to rotate memory maps around the room and ask students to add to, develop and amend each others work. At the centre of each map should be an examination question in order to avoid a purely knowledge based approach to revision as it ensures the content is applied to the requirements of the question as opposed to merely being a regurgitation of facts. A useful technique is to ask the group to remove the question from the centre of the memory map before it is passed to another group and simply ask the group to determine the original question. This use of memory maps also acts as a planning aide and with practice students will complete their maps with sufficient speed to be able to repeat the process within the examination itself.

10. *Quizzes*: Quizzes are always fun and popular especially where prizes are involved. With a plethora of game shows on the many digital channels there is no shortage of ideas which can be copied to make quizzes contemporary and fun. To reduce preparation time for the teacher, ask the students to prepare the questions

while you get creative by thinking which game show to copy. This is where interactive handsets as discussed in Chapter One are a huge asset to a department

---

Chapter summary

Revision can be captivating especially when the whole class are involved in working together and supporting each other's learning. Using as many revision strategies as possible will keep students alert and thinking in a potentially dull and repetitive learning environment. Introducing a new area of knowledge and content during revision can create a more engaging atmosphere but the emphasis should remain on consolidation of learning and application of knowledge and understanding. Revision will be more straightforward if the course content was originally taught in a captivating way.

Pupils cannot be taught simply to think. They have to have something to think about. If this 'something' is trivial, irrelevant or out of date then the education process will be devalued and impoverished. After the novelty of the initial pedagogic adventure, students will lose interest. And of course formulaic approaches, no matter how active and engaging, can soon lose that sense of adventure.

David Lambert, Geographical Association, 2008

In Chapter Two and again in Chapter Four you were asked the question: 'What do you want 'A' Level students to be able to do and to have achieved by the end of their course?' Your students will leave your classroom at the end of their A2 studies having experienced upto 13 years in the education system. Their time with you may have been a fraction of their whole schooling experience but hopefully you will have made an impact on their learning and their lives. Will students leave your tutelage masters of your subject and able to accomplish the skills you set out to develop? Do they have the necessary attributes to support them on the next part of their educational or vocational journey? Are you satisfied that you and they have had a positive learning experience irrespective of the examination results?

This chapter intends to reflect upon the main points from the previous chapters and consider how we can prepare our students for what lies beyond the educational establishment they have been a part of for so many years.

30. The perfect student

Hopefully the perfect student does not exist but some very interesting individual young people come very close to it. Story books are full of man-made creatures built to reflect the perfect qualities desire and usually they become monstrosities of their intended image. Teachers do not set out to create clones and monsters but they do hope to prepare young people for adulthood and in the aims of the 2008 National Curriculum develop their ability to be: 'successful learners, confident individuals and responsible citizens'. These students are our future workers, academics, businessmen, professionals and artistes; their world will be very different to the one we currently live in and their opportunities for success will be enhanced by an ability to be able to think and act for themselves. This does mean that we turn education into a taught set of skills without any knowledge base, this would create a cultural and 'intellectual vacuum' (Lambert 2008). Each worker, academic, businessman and professional requires a subject base to support their understanding and build a platform of change. Our 'A' Level students deserve an intellectual education and a tool kit of learning skills to allow them to continue their education in their own way and at their own pace.

What makes up this intellectual education and a tool kit of learning skills?

♦ Rigorous subject knowledge and understanding.
♦ Independent learning skills.
♦ Ability to make an informed judgement.
♦ Self-motivation.
♦ Breadth of cultural awareness to compliment and challenge subject knowledge.
♦ Challenge.
♦ Self-esteem.
♦ Confidence.
♦ Social and emotional literacy.
♦ Reflective learning skills.
♦ Communication skills.

This is a vast and incomplete list but it gives a flavour of the many agendas under a teachers' jurisdiction in an 'A' Level classroom. It is possible to strive to achieve all of the qualities on the list as long as they are viewed as a long-term goal and not a check list of success. They are aims not objectives and by using a combination of the strategies suggested in the book the list need not be overwhelming.

Enlivened teaching and learning strategies will help students to enjoy their subject first and the learning process second. As a history teacher my goal remains to instil in my students a life long appreciation of their past and a passion for history in the future. A mathematics teacher will also wish to instil a love of the problematic and infinite challenge of numbers. If we care for our subject this enthusiasm will transfer to the classroom; if we jump through examination built hoops it will destroy any sense of individual subject relevance and identity.

By making every second in the classroom count the students will look forward to their time with you and will hold it in their memories. Give yourself the opportunity to experiment with learning styles and techniques in the classroom. Select appropriately for your subject and consider how that approach to learning more than any other will support the demands of your subject needs. If an activity does not go as planned; reflect upon why not with your students; this will engage students in the learning process and help you and them the next time you try a similar activity. Use the students' maturity and ability to your advantage to make lessons interesting and thought-provoking without having to dwell too much on issues relating to behaviour management.

Encouraging students to be independent will be of immense benefit to their further education learning needs and in the employment market. Students will have to make informed and independent decisions as adults as well as manage their own time and if we do not equip them for this we are failing them. By telling students what to do, think, say and write, we are reducing their capacity to function on their own. This route to independence will require signposts and pit stops but they will get there with your help.

Assessment for learning will underpin most of the previous list of student attributes. Regular reflection on progress and how to improve will arm you and the students with a self-awareness of their own learning achievements as well as help them to determine what they need to do to get better. At post-16 their incentive may be a pre-determined grade but their learning journey along the way will teach them more than how to reach their target grade. Not only will the assessment for learning techniques discussed build reflective learners they will also make lessons and the production of assignments and tasks interesting and purposeful. So many times we ask students to complete work without questioning why we are asking them to do it. The note taking lesson discussed in Chapter One could be more interesting simply by being given a purpose. Always ask the question: 'Why am I asking students to complete a given task?' If it is because the scheme of work says so return to your lesson objectives and ask again: 'Why am I asking the students to do this task in this way?' The answer to this question will give your lesson a purpose which will be conveyed to the students through your lesson objectives and make for a more rigorous lesson for all.

Creating an inclusive classroom can be challenging. A point repeatedly raised though this book has been the diverse nature of the students you teach and the issues this presents. Teaching to the most-able can exclude those who find every lesson difficult. Offering opportunities within and outside your classroom to the most-able will stimulate and invigorate their enthusiasm for their studies and engage them in areas they may have otherwise found dull. Know your class first and present tasks early in the course that will give the most-able an opportunity to reveal their potential and plan accordingly from this point using ideas from Chapter Four.

Preparing students for their final examination is essential and students benefit from familiarity with the examination content and process. Revision can be made engaging through appealing to their interests and curiosity. Ask questions and let the students find the answers. Make the examination non-threatening and an opportunity to look forward to when students can finally show off all they have learned. With independent learning skills in place students will be in a position to take full advantage of any study leave that is available to them.

Summary

The perfect student is a young person who has enjoyed their AS or A2 course, has a desire to learn, can ask questions when needing help and gets the grade they are deserve for a future they are worthy of.

31. Role of parents and carers

In post-16 education finding the equilibrium between engendering independence and involving parent and carer (referred to as parent for the remainder of the section) support can be problematic. Students wish to have an increased sense of liberation from their parents in many aspects of their lives including their academic or vocational ventures. Yet their parents wish to be involved in their children's achievements and progress. In the most part parents wish to be supportive of their children's education and do everything they can to ensure their children receive the opportunities that are available to them. Parents can often feel they are only contacted if there is a problem and can feel removed from the daily lives of their children. They can also feel alienated by the nature of the study and content itself which may be far removed form their own educational experiences. This alienation need not be the case and parents can work in partnership with Sixth Form or college and offer the external support to help your students meet the goals you have determined for them as well as reach for the aspiration they have set themselves.

In a school Sixth Form situation this can be easier to accomplish as there will be a legacy of a parental involvement and relationships between the school and home will already have been nurtured. In a college environment this will be more difficult due to the fluid nature of a students' college day and the number of students involved in a college system. As a teacher it may feel inappropriate or even go against protocol to contact parents on an individual basis but there are ways of creating home-class links which can work to the advantage of all involved. Below are a series of suggestions for increased home-class contact which can work to the benefit of the student without reducing the autonomy of the student over their school life.

◆ Set an out of class task which has to be completed with parental involvement. For example, ask the student to teach a new concept or subject-specific phrase to their parent and ask the parent to feedback on how confident they feel in passing on the same information to someone else.
◆ Ask the student to share their first set of feedback and target setting with their parent and ask the parent to make a positive comment in regard to the student's achievements.
◆ Use reward systems to praise individual contributions from students and directly inform the parent that their child is 'global geographer' 'mathematician of the moment' or other subject-specific award. Students can elect their own 'student of the month' based on class agreed criteria.
◆ Invite parents to a class exhibition of work after a parents' evening. Use regular work not specially created materials to exemplify what students do on a regular basis.

◆ Have a parents week on the VLE and ask students to encourage their parents to make a comment, observation or contribution to the forum debate.

◆ Ask if parents can contribute anything to the course in terms of their own experience and knowledge. As courses become increasingly specialized parents will have their own expertise they can share with the class. The student may be embarrassed by Dad turning up to class but if the rest of the class gain from the experience the discomfort will pass.

Summary

Parental involvement is more than a monitoring exercise that students are doing their work outside of class and being punished if they are not. It provides an opportunity for parents to share in the achievements and growth of their child. Many parents will be amazed at the range and breadth of their child's education and be delighted to receive guidance on how to support their child's education further. There is a wealth of untapped parental talent and expertise available to teachers and if we recognize the value of outside experts in advancing students education where better to start than at home.

32. Key skills

Key skills have been briefly addressed in Chapter One. They are an area of our students' education that can be compartmentalized by staff and students and leave subject teachers unaware of how they can maximize students' key skills opportunities. This section will explore each of the components of key skills in more depth and how they can be applied into everyday lessons. Key skills are an integral part of programmes at key stage 4, post-16 and of modern apprenticeships. Young people may be working towards key skills qualifications, using the wider key skills units to support their learning, or developing their key skills without aiming for qualifications. Schools and colleges tend to have their own approach to delivering key skills and with the introduction of diplomas, are making links with functional skills. Institutions that are most satisfied with their approach have established a clear policy with designated staff responsible for working alongside subject teachers as well as acting as internal moderators. Some schools and colleges are linked to key skills centres to support students with all aspects of key skills.

There are six key skills:

◆ *Application of Number*: Interpreting information involving numbers, carrying out calculations, interpreting results and presenting findings
◆ *Communication*: Speaking, listening, reading and writing skills
◆ *Information Technology*: Finding, exploring, developing and presenting information including text, images and numbers.

These first three key skills are sometimes referred to as the 'main' key skills as they incorporate the basic skills of literacy, numeracy and ICT. The remaining three are often referred to as the 'wider' or 'soft' key skills due to their less tangible and more abstract nature.

◆ *Improving Own Learning and Performance*: Developing independent learners who are clearly focused on what they want to achieve and able to work towards targets that will improve the quality of their learning and performance. The standards include process skills, for example, target-setting, planning, learning, reviewing and interpersonal skills, for example, communicating own needs, accepting constructive feedback, negotiating learning opportunities and support.
◆ *Problem Solving*: Encouraging learners to develop and demonstrate their ability to tackle problems systematically, for the purpose of working towards their solution and learning from this process. Three types or combinations of problems are dealt with: diagnostic problems that depend primarily on analysis to arrive at conclusions, design problems that depend mainly on synthesis to create a product or process, and contingency problems that typically involve resource planning and gaining the cooperation of others, for example, when organizing an event
◆ *Working with Others*: Process and interpersonal skills to support working cooperatively with others to achieve shared objectives, work cooperatively and have regard for others.

Some schools and colleges have integrated key skills development into their schemes of work, and in these institutions inspections have found that staff and students find the key skills work relevant. If departments are able to map the key skills requirements against those of a subject teaching programme, teachers can identify where key skills teaching will enhance subject teaching. Skills that are not developed as a natural part of students' subject learning can be developed in discrete classes. Students can also use key skills accreditation as part of their UCAS points score but some higher education institutions are uneasy about their use, so always ask students to check. For many teachers key skills are imposed and for others they are not aware of them. As an individual teacher issues relating to the implementation of key skills are largely out of your control. An awareness of their role and value can only be beneficial to the students on your course. Encourage the class to be proactive in seeking openings in lessons to achieve their levels rather than waiting for you to present the opportunities to them, reinforcing the importance of independent learning further.

QCA's view on helping students to understand the importance of key skills

To help students understand the value of developing their key skills and taking key skills qualifications, schools and colleges are:

◆ creating a clear expectation that all students will develop their key skills;
◆ ensuring that all staff promote the value of key skills;
◆ encouraging staff to develop their own key skills;
◆ assuring students that appropriate key skills acquisition will support their subject work, improve grades and not prove an extra burden;
◆ offering a choice of key skills and approach;
◆ pointing out that even when key skills are not stated as a requirement for an HE course, an applicant with evidence of key skills may have an advantage;
◆ emphasizing that students who have completed one or more key skills qualifications at the end of Year 12 have

UCAS points to declare on their application forms alongside AS. (The UCAS tariff recognizes key skills achievement at levels 2, 3 and 4; level 4 = 30 UCAS points, level 2 = 10 UCAS points);

♦ pointing out that HEIs are also involved in key skills development.

Summary

Key skills are a means to create greater breadth in all our students. The Diploma system being introduced in 2008 reinforces this breadth with their own emphasis on functional skills to extend a student's numeracy, literacy and ICT capabilities. The expectation by futures analysts is that future employment will be more highly skilled than ever before and in a competitive work market students will require 'higher level of skills and more qualifications' (LSC). Whether fuelled by a political agenda or a desire to help students learn there is a benefit in key skills for all students and through working towards level 4 in all components students can make their own classroom more captivating.

33. Where next?

Within months of students embarking upon their AS courses they have to begin considering not only what they will pursue at A2 level but what their post-18 options are as well. Colleges and schools have access to in-house or local authority careers advisers to offer expert advice on the options available to students. Schools and colleges are kept informed of reputable websites and information packs can help students make informed choices about their future. Tutors work with students to help them write a personal statement and through the application procedure for employment or higher education. As a subject teacher you may contribute to their personal statement and reference through report writing and tracking procedures.

Students may ask your advice on where to study your subject. This is always very flattering and for some new teachers fresh from their own higher education experience relatively easy to answer. However for some teachers who graduated many years previously this can be a difficult question to answer and expert advice is required. Consult with younger staff who will have a much greater wealth of knowledge to draw on and if possible ask them to share some of their higher education experiences with students.

In relation to employment in your own subject area consider what your undergraduate associates went on to do. Where did their specialist degrees take them and what attributes did the chosen degree equip them with? Subject associations often have data and information relating to their subject post degree and which vocational or professional route graduates chose to take. Trips and visits can expose students to a wealth of subject expertise and opportunities within their chosen subject. Again look to parents and personal friends to share their professional knowledge and experience in relation to recruitment.

'Aimhigher' provide university access days for students especially young people who have no tradition of attending university. Local university open days can provide an early experience of a university even if is not the one of choice. By providing opportunities to talk with other adults, hear individual stories and visit work places you will be raising aspirations and opening new horizons. For many students their view of the adult world is shaped by their parent's experiences and expectations. In a global society the opportunities available to young people are more exciting than ever and simply talking about different possibilities and options can trigger an interest in an area previously unbeknown to them.

Summary

You are not expected to be an expert in careers advice but again as an AS and A2 teacher it is helpful to know where students can seek advice from. Raising awareness of the world of higher education and employment within your classroom can in turn raise students' aspirations. Merely widening students' horizons is valuable as an end in itself.

34. Conclusions

*All too often we are giving young people cut flowers when we should
be teaching them to grow their own plants. We are stuffing their heads
with the products of earlier innovation rather than teaching them to
innovate. We think of the mind as a storehouse to be filled when we
should be thinking of it as an instrument to be used.*

John Gardner, 1973

'A' level teaching is stimulating, varied, challenging and exciting.
You have the chance to work with young people who are on the brink
of adulthood and looking to their own futures with enthusiasm,
anticipation and trepidation. As their teacher they will look to you for
knowledge, expertise, guidance and support. It may at times become
overwhelming to attempt to meet the many agendas of post-16
education and lesson planning may appear to be a checklist of
initiatives and criteria. It is important to remember that the learning
drives a good lesson and your subject expertise, awareness of the
syllabus and educational beliefs are the agendas that determine how
you teach and your students learn.

An 'A' Level classroom can be a captivating place for young people
to discover and learn, a place where they can feel confident, secure,
challenged, fascinated and filled with curiosity.

References and further reading

References are cited for their first appearance though they may be referred to in other chapters.

Chapter one

Brooks V., Abbott I. and Bills L. (2004), *Preparing to Teach In Secondary Schools*. Maidenhead: Open University Press.

Ginnis P. (2002), *The Teacher's Toolkit*. Carmarthean: Crown House Publishing.

Graddol D., Maybin J. and Stierer B. (1993), *Researching Language and Literacy In Social Context*. Maidenhead: Open University Press.

Norman K. (1992), *Thinking Voices: Work of the National Oracy Project*. London: Hodder Arnold H&S.

Office for Standards in Education (OfSTED) (2003), *Book for Inspecting Secondary Schools*.

Smith S. and Piele P. (2006), *School Leadership: Handbook for Excellence in Student Learning* (Fourth edition). Thousand Oaks, CA: Corwin Press.

Drapeau P. (2009), *Differentiating With Graphic Organizers Tools to Foster Critical and Creative Thinking*. Thousand Oaks, CA: Sage Publications.

Online references

http://www.standards.dfes.gov.uk/secondary/keystage3/

http://www.ocr.org.uk/qualifications/1419changes/alevels/index.html#list

http://www.edexcel.com/gce2008/Pages/Overview.aspx

http://www.aqa.org.uk/qual/gce.php

http://www.qca.org.uk/14-19/11-16-schools/index_s5-3-using-key-skills.htm

Chapter two

Culpin C. (2002), Why we must change history at GCSE. *Teaching History*, Vol. 109.

Lee P. and Shemilt D. (2003), A Scaffold Not a Cage. *Teaching History*, Vol. 113.

O'Doherty M. (2006), *Learn Higher*. Manchester: The University of Manchester.

Wallace B. (2003), *Using History to Develop Thinking Skills at Key Stage 2*.

London: David Fulton Publishers (A NACE-Fulton Pub) ISBN 1 85346 928 9

Wallace B. (2002), *Teaching Thinking Skills Across the Early Years*.

London: David Fulton Publishers (A NACE-Fulton Pub) ISBN 1 85346 842 8

Wallace B (2002), *Teaching Thinking Skills Across the Middle Years*.

London: David Fulton Publishers (A NACE-Fulton Pub) ISBN 1 85346 767 7

Wallace B. (2001), *Teaching Thinking Skills Across the Primary Curriculum*.

London: David Fulton Publishers (A NACE-Fulton Pub) ISBN 1 85346 766 9

Wallace B. and Maker J., et al. (2004), *Thinking Skills and Problem-Solving: An Inclusive Approach*. London: David Fulton Publishers (A NACE-Fulton Pub) ISBN 1 84312 107 7

Walker, S. and Chadbourne, J. (2006), *TULIP – A Strategy for the Development of Independent Learning*.

Online references

http://www.brookes.ac.uk/schools/education/rescon/case-studies/birdwellmalinardone.pdf

http://www.nace.co.uk/

http://curriculum.qca.org.uk/key-stages-3-and-4/skills/plts/index.aspx?return=/key-stages-3-and-4/skills/index.aspxNational

http://www.nationalarchives.gov.uk/

www.dfes.gov.uk/personalisedlearning

www.teachernet.gov.uk/publications/

www.dfes.gov.uk/14-19

Chapter three

Stahl R. (1994), Using 'Think-Time' and 'Wait-Time' Skillfully in the Classroom. *ERIC Digest*.

Husbands C. (1996), *What is History Teaching?* Buckingham: Open University Press.

Assessment for Learning: 10 Principles Assessment Reform Group (2002).

OfSTED (2003), Good Assessment in Secondary Schools

Black P. and Wiliam D. (1998), *Inside the Black Box Raising Standards Through Classroom Assessment*. London: School of Education, Kings College.

Black P., Harrison C., Lee C., Marshall B. and Wiliam D. (2003) *Assessment for Learning – Putting it into Practice*. Maidenhead: Open University Press.

Clarke S. (2005), *Formative Assessment in the Secondary Classroom*. London: Hodder Murray.

Kryiacou C. (1997), *Effective Teaching In Schools Theory and Practice*. Cheltonham: Nelson Thornes.

Gardner J. (2006), *Assessment and Learning*. Sage publications.

Gilbert C. (2007), *2020 Vision – Naace position paper*. London: QCA Secondary Curriculum Review.

Online references

http://www.qca.org.uk/qca_4334.aspxCurriculum 2000

Chapter four

Barnes S. (2007), *Meeting the Needs of Your Most Able Pupils*. Abingdon, Oxon: David Fulton.

Leat D. (2000), *Thinking Through Series*. Cambridge: Chris Kington Publishing.

Evans L. (January 2008), *Gifted and Talented Update*. London: Optimus publishing.

Evans L. (June 2007), *Gifted and Talented Update*. London: Optimus publishing.

Evans L. and Bulmer M. (September 2006), *Gifted and Talented Update*. Optimus publishing.

DCSF *Leading Teacher Handbook*.

Brooks V., Abbott I. and Bills L. (2004), *Preparing to Teach in Secondary Schools*. Maidenhead: Open University Press.

Ginnis P. (2002), *The Teacher's Toolkit*. Carmarthean: Crown House Publishing.

Eyre D. (2005), Expertise in its development phase. *Teaching History*, Vol. 124.

DCSF (2006), *Learning Outside the Classroom Manifesto*.

DCSF *Guidance on Effective Provision for Gifted and Talented*.

Online references

DCSF Gifted and Talented. http://www.standards.dfes.gov.uk/giftedandtalented/

CfBT Gifted and Talented. http://www.cfbt.com/teach/localauthorities/giftedtalentededucation.aspx

Young Gifted and Talented. http://ygt.dcsf.gov.uk/?stakeholder=14

Villiers Park Education Trust. http://www.villierspark.org.uk/vphome.php

Aimhigher. www.aimhigher.ac.uk

NACE. http://www.nace.co.uk/

Key to Success. https://www.keytosuccess.dfes.gov.uk/

Chapter five

See other chapters.

Chapter six

Lambert D. (2008), *Opinion Piece – Why Subjects Really Matter, A Personal View*. Sheffield: Geographical Association.

Gardner J. (1973), In *The Changing Classroom* Goodell, C. (ed.), Versatility and innovation. New York: Ballantine, pp. 117–118.

Online references

LSC. http://inourhands.lsc.gov.uk/aboutus.html

Connexions Careers advice. http://www.connexions-direct.com

Aimhigher. http://www.teachernet.gov.uk/aimhigher/

Index